RAT TERRIER

A COMPLETE AND RELIABLE HANDBOOK

Linda Hibbard

RX-133

CONTENTS

THE RAT TERRIER

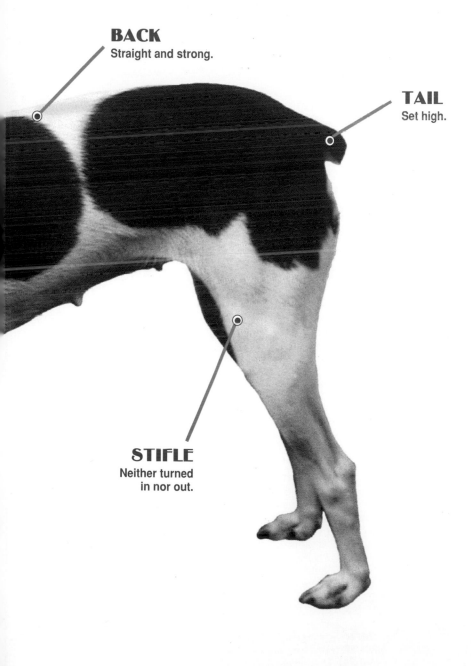

BACK
Straight and strong.

TAIL
Set high.

STIFLE
Neither turned
in nor out.

Title Page: Rat Terrier photographed by Isabelle Francais.

Photographers: Anne Blair, Barbara Castro, Walter D. Dickison, Dennis Eiland, Isabelle Francais, Jayle Goucher, Carson Hibbard, Linda Hibbard, Noel Hibbard, Ralph B. Jackson.

© **by T.F.H. Publications, Inc.**

Distributed in the UNITED STATES to the Pet Trade by T.F.H. Publications, Inc., One T.F.H. Plaza, Neptune City, NJ 07753; distributed in the UNITED STATES to the Bookstore and Library Trade by National Book Network, Inc. 4720 Boston Way, Lanham MD 20706; in CANADA to the Pet Trade by H & L Pet Supplies Inc., 27 Kingston Crescent, Kitchener, Ontario N2B 2T6; Rolf C. Hagen Inc., 3225 Sartelon St. Laurent-Montreal Quebec H4R 1E8; in CANADA to the Book Trade by Vanwell Publishing Ltd., 1 Northrup Crescent, St. Catharines, Ontario L2M 6P5 ; in ENGLAND by T.F.H. Publications, PO Box 15, Waterlooville PO7 6BQ; in AUSTRALIA AND THE SOUTH PACIFIC by T.F.H. (Australia), Pty. Ltd., Box 149, Brookvale 2100 N.S.W., Australia; in NEW ZEALAND by Brooklands Aquarium Ltd. 5 McGiven Drive, New Plymouth, RD1 New Zealand; in Japan by T.F.H. Publications, Japan—Jiro Tsuda, 10-12-3 Ohjidai, Sakura, Chiba 285, Japan; in SOUTH AFRICA by Lopis (Pty) Ltd., P.O. Box 39127, Booysens, 2016, Johannesburg, South Africa. Published by T.F.H. Publications, Inc.

MANUFACTURED IN THE
UNITED STATES OF AMERICA
BY T.F.H. PUBLICATIONS, INC.

THE ORIGIN AND HISTORY OF THE RAT TERRIER

The old-fashioned Rat Terrier originated in England in the 1820s. He was a cross between the Smooth Fox Terrier and the black and tan Manchester Terrier. The crossing of the two breeds produced a hardy, tenacious, small varmint dog with the consistent coloring of the Manchester (a black body and face with tan spots over the eyes and on each cheek).

THE RAT TERRIER: A FEIST
All Rat Terriers are feists, but not all feists are Rat Terriers. Our primary interest is in the history and the development of the Rat Terrier. In order to understand this breed, we need to know his ancestry. It is interesting to understand the Rat Terrier's lineage and how he evolved from the "Feist" strain in England.

The Rat Terrier was originally known as a "Feist" due to his hardy and tenacious demeanor.

The Toy Fox Terrier, shown here, is just one of the ancestors in the mixed heritage of the Rat Terrier.

As stated previously, it was during the 1820s that the English began crossing the Fox Terrier with the Manchester Terrier. The resulting hybrid proved to be nothing short of spectacular. The combination of the genes produced a superior terrier to either the Fox or the Manchester. The hybrid's parents were both "tenacious and feisty" and because of these traits, they came to be known by the English as "feists."

It didn't take long for word to travel about the little hybrid and his versatility. Within a few years they were well known and extremely popular throughout Great Britain. The Feist became popular for his work in pit baiting and many became champions in the art of rat killing.

One of the most popular sports in England was to place a Feist in a pit and then pour hundreds of rats on top of the dog. Betting took place on which dog would kill the most rats. The contests were not only popular with the huntsmen, but were avid social events of the times. The popularity of the Feist grew enormously. Over the next 60 years, the dog was more or less confined to the geographical location of Great Britain.

Many changes were to take place in the Feist strain in the 1890s. It was the Americans who went to England and exported the Feist to the United States. The hybrid dog was to undergo a period of refinement, thus making him more of an utility dog. The process of change in the dogs' breeding was to lessen the breed's hunting characteristics, thereby producing dogs with a more adaptable personality. Changes were to continue in Feist breeding until the final adjustments occurred in the 1930s. The final result would birth an American breed, known today as the Rat Terrier.

Change was inevitable. Our forefathers faced many dangers and hardships in frontier life, and their animals were an integral part of their survival. The early settlers had brought various types of dogs with them when our country was first settled. These canine friends assisted in taming the dangers of the wilderness. The expectations of these men who brought the Feists from England were an outgrowth of the traits of the generations of dogs that they had hunted with in years past. Gone were the years of conquest. America was becoming both settled and civilized. Hunters no longer needed the large, strong, cur types that could protect the home from marauding bears, cougars, and their like.

Developed to trail and tree small game, today's Rat Terrier still retains these hunting instincts. Flame, owned by Dennis Eiland, chases a squirrel up a tree in his backyard.

At the turn of the 19th century, the desired dog was one that could excel in trailing and treeing small game. It was hoped that breeding in more blood of the Smooth Fox Terrier would produce a dog more suited to the needs of the time. The goal was to propagate better hunting dogs.

The result of the addition of the Smooth Fox Terrier was to alter the personality of the hybrid, toning down his rough aggressive traits. The breeding was not exactly perfect and it was to leave the Feist with some loss of his distinctiveness. Dennis Eiland, noted writer and author on the Rat Terrier, states, "What had been a 50-50 cross of two strains was not a strain of a Fox Terrier. The percentage breakdown was 80% Fox Terrier, 20% Manchester. The last 10 to 20% increase of Fox Terrier infusion was an experimental effort at trying to increase desired hunting characteristics. This objective wasn't achieved; however, the traits that were present were stabilized. The fanciers of these dogs refused to believe that the traits that were lacking could not somehow be bred in. Thus they began to look at other small breeds of hunting dogs for possible infusion of those traits."

Feest, faust, fyste, fice, and feist are the spellings given by the *American Dialect Dictionary*, defining the word as a small snarling dog, a small disagreeable dog, and an undersized vicious dog. *Webster's Dictionary* describes Feist as being "simply a small dog." The earliest recorded usage of the word in America dates back to 1890 in Kentucky. In a 1913 issue of *Our Southern Highlanders*, a North Carolina bear hunter describes the Feists as "one o' them little bitty dogs that generally run around on three legs and pretends a whole lot." It's not surprising to learn that the Feist has several different terriers in his background and has been bred for his natural hunting instincts. The Feist can be any color; some are brindle, but most are a mixture of the hound colors—white, black, tan, and lemon. They are a short-haired dog, well proportioned, and weigh between 10 and 30 pounds. The dog should not exceed 18 inches in height. Their tails can be docked or left natural; some Fiests are born with bobtails. Most carry their tails curled over their back and some have hind dewclaws and a denser coat than others. These Asiatic traits were inherited from the native American spitz-type dogs that were crossed with the 1890 Feist Terriers. The Rat Terrier is preferred to have a docked tail in the typical terrier fashion; that is between the second and third joint. When a Rat Terrier is born with a natural bobtail, however, it should be left alone. Other common characteristics between the Rat Terrier and the Feist are that they both have somewhat pointed noses and should have ears that are set high on their heads, either held erect, semi-pricked (tulip), or dropped forward (button).

The Feist has always been known as an intelligent, bold, and aggressive dog with high endurance. In the woods he should have a short to medium hunting range, always circling his territory rather than hunting in a straight line. He should possess a strong treeing instinct and a hot nose (that is, only trail tracks that are fresh, rather than wasting his time cold trailing). He needs to be alert, hunting his game with eyes, ears, and nose.

The Feist, in general, is unequaled as a small game hunter. He is also a good yard dog and a fine house

One common characteristic between the Rat Terrier and the Feist is the dog's head—both have long pointed noses and high-set ears.

pet. His ancestors more than likely originated in Europe, having been brought to America by the early settlers. Perhaps the American Indians also kept small gaming-type dogs as hunters and pets. They probably bred with European stock to produce the forerunners of the Feists that exist today.

Presently, one of the most important challenges facing Feist breeders and fanciers is strengthening the hunting characteristics of the breed. Improvement can only be accomplished by being more selective in the choice of dogs that will be used for breeding stock.

The Feist has re-established himself as a much sought after breed in recent years, especially in the southern United States. Because these dogs are strong, lively, and easy to keep up, they are rapidly becoming a very popular breed.

The Rat Terrier (Feist) has been a distinct breed for almost 100 years. Depending on the geographical location, Rat Terriers also have been long referred to as Smooth Fox Terriers and it is recognized that the Rat Terrier "strain" was derived from the Smooth Fox Terrier. The Rat Terrier is recognized by the Universal Kennel Club International (UKCI). UKCI was the first kennel club to register the Rat Terrier and is the largest and most complete registry for the breed. The Toy Fox Terrier and Amatory, like other Toy breeds, are offspring of the standard size Smooth Fox Terrier.

HISTORY OF THE TOY FOX TERRIER (RAT TERRIER)

The Toy Fox Terrier is an offshoot of the standard size Fox Terrier and the Old English Fox Terrier is the grandfather of all modern day breeds of terriers. The standard-size Fox Terrier was discovered in England prior to 1864. From his ancestry came the Irish, Fox, Welsh, and Airedale Terriers. The above dogs were known for their proficiency in hunting fox, badger, weasel, foulmart, and water rats. The larger dogs weighed between 7 and 30 pounds. The smaller runts weighed less than seven pounds. The Toy Fox Terrier weighed three and one-half to seven pounds.

The Rat Terrier is not only a tough working dog but can be a loving addition to any family. Carson Hibbard with his dogs Bridget and puppy Hercules.

In order to propagate the breed, the Rat Terrier was crossed with other breeds of dog, including the Manchester Terrier, shown here.

It was from the strain of the Old English Fox Terrier and the standard-size Fox Terrier that other breeds of terriers such as the Bedlington, Border (1920), Bull (1835), Cairn, Dandie Dinmont (1706), Kerry Blue, Lakeland, Norwich (1800), Scottish (1561), and Sealyham (1891) were to originate in England, Ireland, and Scotland. These various terriers had different hunting instincts. Various degrees of hunting abilities were bred into the hybrid dogs so that they could be of value in their locality. The Manchester Terrier has the prestigious distinction of being the first toy breed to have been developed and the breed is most important to the development of the Rat Terrier.

Fox Terriers are without a doubt the best known of all breeds of Terriers; their ancestors were no mystery to the English. The genetic makeup of the Fox Terrier includes the English Black and Tan, Bull Terrier, Italian Greyhound, and Beagle.

BREED OR STRAIN?

According to Dennis Eiland, "...many dogs were bred for the poorman's sport of bullbaiting. These dogs were commonly crosses of Bulldog and Terrier mixes. When the sport was outlawed during the 1830s, the betting sports of the den "pits" were insti-

Trailing and treeing is a sport in which the Rat Terrier excels and still participates in today. Trevor Wallace with Dennis Eiland's Rat Terriers.

tuted. Snap dogs (rabbit catching/coursing), ratting, and (dog) pit fighting contests were the entertainment of the miners and poor people of the times (1830-1890). Today many of these sporting terrier breeds are still referred to generically as ratters."

At the turn of the century, many breeds were developed, primarily due to the advent of The Kennel Club in England in 1876. Prior to The Kennel Club, only royalty and landed gentry could exhibit livestock. Gradually, the emerging English middle class was permitted to have dog shows. (Today dogs are still shown "stacked" as sheep are.) Small dogs, toy dogs, and unusual dogs were in vogue, and dog shows were to become the rage.

New breeds of dogs were created, developed, and refined over the past 150 years by cross breeding various types and strains. Breed standards were written to describe the "ideal" dog. Technically any breed without a breed standard is considered to be a strain. Until recently, the Rat Terrier had been without a breed standard and therefore had not been recognized as a breed, but rather as a strain. Also, little had been written about this strain of the Smooth Fox Terrier, again, probably because the breed went without a standard for so long.

The Rat Terrier has existed in America's farming heartlands, hardwood forests, and mountain areas for decades, however, the strain differed from one geographical location to the next. There were literally hundreds of small breeding communities throughout the United States. Breeders had been left on their own to develop the type of dog that best suited their needs and likes.

The Toy Fox Terrier originated from the Rat Terrier (1910-1920) and the Rat Terrier strain was developed from the Feist/Manchester/Smooth Fox Terrier crosses of the 1890s. Thus for almost a century these "ratters" existed. History tells us that many dogs were destroyed because they were mismarked, or had too much or not enough white.

Most of the breeders preferred mating Rat Terrier to Rat Terrier. Often, individuals had little knowledge of what other breeders were doing. At this time, we must remember that no breed standard existed. This, coupled with the unavailability of extensive breeding stock, produced variations both in size and weight.

Seven-month-old Sissy owned by W. Dean Dickison is a wonderful example of a liver-and-white Rat Terrier.

Until recently there was cross breeding in the Rat Terrier lines. Rat Terriers were crossed with Toy Fox Terriers, Manchester Terriers, and Chihuahuas, as well as other breeds. These cross breedings were not only warranted, but necessary for the survival of the breed. Today, it is no longer necessary.

As of January 1, 1998, the Universal Kennel Club International officially has refused to register any dog that has been cross bred as a Rat Terrier. Any dog that has been crossed with another breed will be considered a hybrid.

The UKCI has officially adopted the breed standard of the National Rat Terrier Association as the standard of the breed, and does not recommend or accept any cross breedings with the Rat Terrier as being a purebred Rat Terrier.

THE RAT TERRIER IN THE UNITED STATES

The Rat Terrier, at that time known as a Feist, was first introduced into the United States in the 1890s. It was Theodore Roosevelt, the 26th President, who was responsible for naming the little hybrid the "Rat Terrier."

When the President moved into the White House in 1901, it was infested with rats. Traps and various poisons were planted throughout the mansion, all to no avail. The President owned several of the small Feist-type dogs, and he let them loose in his living quarters. Within hours the dogs had killed numerous vermin. Fittingly, Roosevelt dubbed the small Feist the "Rat Terrier," which is synonymous with his other name, the "Squirrel Dog."

Theodore Roosevelt loved animals, and he especially loved his Rat Terriers. Skip was the President's favorite dog, a Rat Terrier that he acquired when he went on a trip to the Grand Canyon. The President said, "Skip was a good hunter and fighter and would stand his ground before a bear or a lynx at bay. But Skip was also a loving little dog." He would sometimes get tired on the trail, jump into the President's lap, and ride on the saddle with Theodore Roosevelt.

Skip was also fond of the President's son's horse, Algonquin. He loved to play with the horse. He enjoyed running along side Algonquin, then jumping onto his back. Archie, the President's son, loved having races with Skip. They would run and play on the second floor of the White House. He enjoyed a happy life and died in 1907.

Other Rat Terriers that occupied the White House were Allen, owned by Roosevelt's son Kermit; Gem, who was owned by Edith Roosevelt; and Peter, Black Jack, and Scamp—all family dogs.

It was in the United States that major changes took place in the developmental breeding of the Rat Terrier. Through selective breeding, additional blood of the Smooth Fox Terrier was added into the strain, producing differences in the coloring of the Feist. His color changed from predominately black and tan, which mostly resembled the Manchester, to that of the typical Fox Terrier, which is black and white or brown and white.

As time passed, breeders added Beagle and Italian Greyhound into the lineage of the Feist. The Beagle's colors, which are the same as the Rat's, had little, if any, effect on the color of the dog.

Greyhounds, with so many varied colors and patterns, made a profound change on the color of the Feist. As a result of cross breeding with the Greyhound, Rat Terriers now come in many colors, the most common being black and tan on white, which is accepted as the standard color of the breed. The dogs also come in various colors of tan, liver, brown, red, apricot, and blue. It is not uncommon for the Rat Terrier to be almost totally white in color; even more rare is solid red or brindle. Some breeders produce Rats that have the original colors of the Manchester. All color variations are proper for the breed with one exception—brindle. It is wise when choosing a Rat Terrier puppy to look for a dog that has sufficient color on the head. Rat Terriers that lack color around their ears are prone to deafness.

Joseph Becchinelli, President of the UKCI, and staff with two Toy Rat Terriers.

RAT TERRIER IN THE UNITED STATES

During the 1950s there was a severe breed decline that left only a handful of breeders in the business. At this time there wasn't a breed standard. Most breeders preferred mating Rat Terrier to Rat Terrier. Often individuals who were breeding had little knowledge of what other breeders were doing. This, coupled with the unavailability of extensive breeding stock, produced both variations in size, and weight. The Universal Kennel Club International's acceptance of offspring of a Rat Terrier mated to either a Toy Fox Terrier, Manchester, or Chihuahua as a Rat Terrier was not only warranted, but necessary for the survival of the breed. Rat Terriers were not indiscriminately bred, but crosses to these few breeds were allowed.

The Scotts, pioneers in the advancement of this strain of Rat Terriers, pose with their group of American Hairless Terriers.

In 1972, a marvelous and historical event took place in Louisiana. A hairless female pup was whelped in a litter of regular, mid-sized Rat Terriers. From the mutation of this litter, the American Hairless Terrier developed. These little hairless dogs are born with fuzz, then start shedding at about six weeks of age until only their eyebrows and whiskers remain. The original hairless pup was named Josephine, and she was owned by Willie and Edwin Scott of Louisiana. Josephine had several different litters. In her first

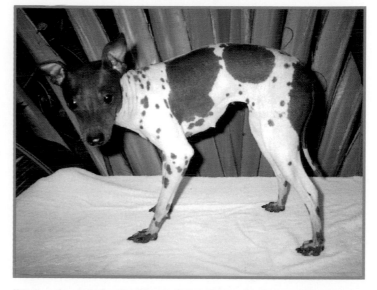

Although they began as a mutation, breeding programs are being established to develop the hairless strain of the Rat Terrier.

litter, she had a hairless female pup. Josephine went on to have several different litters without delivering another hairless pup until her final litter when she produce two hairless, one being a male and the other a female. The last two hairless pups that were born to Josephine became the foundation of a new breeding program. Today there are only about 140 hairless Rat Terriers (American Hairless Terriers) in the world. The Scotts hope to keep the temperament of the Rat Terrier, yet produce dogs that are hairless. The Scotts, along with Robert Earl of Pompano Beach, Florida, are pioneering in the development of this new strain of the Rat Terrier. The Universal Kennel Club International does recognize and register the American Hairless Terrier.

In 1958, the first Rat Terrier was registered with the Universal Kennel Club International. Today there are more than 300,000 registered with that same club, just the tip of the iceberg. The breed is gaining popularity at a furious rate. Much of the breed's popularity is due to the efforts of the Universal Kennel Club International. The goal of the club is to protect, standardize, and inform "Rat lovers" of the wonderful enjoyment one can receive as an owner of a Rat Terrier.

HE HEARS HIS MASTER'S VOICE

The RCA dog pictured on their products is none other than the little Rat Terrier known as Nipper. He gained recognition in 1901 when the Victor Talking Machine Company adopted him as their mascot.

Nipper was born in Bristol, England, in 1884. When his owner died, he went to live with the owner's brother, an artist named Francis Barraud. Barraud played a record on the old-fashioned gramophone and found Nipper listening to the voice. He painted a picture as he saw Nipper listening to the machine and entitled his work, "His Master's Voice." Today Nipper lives on and is recognized as one of the world's most memorable trademarks.

THE NATIONAL RAT TERRIER ASSOCIATION

The National Rat Terrier Association is a club devoted to the growth and development of the Rat Terrier. The NRTA has specific goals that include the organization and promotion of dog shows, not only at the local and regional levels, but at the national level as well. Rat Terriers will be awarded championship points at the various shows thus enabling them to receive championship titles.

Members of the NRTA are encouraged to register their dogs with the Universal Kennel Club International. The UKCI is not only one of the oldest registries of Rat Terriers, but has proven to be the registry most used by quality breeders. By registering with one central registry, we are keeping the rare breed of the Rat Terrier at a central locality. It should be kept in

Perhaps the most well-known Rat Terrier, Nipper, shown here in the painting by Francis Barraud, became the spokesdog for the RCA Company.

The National Rat Terrier Association is committed to the promotion and the continuation of high-quality breeding programs. Hercules owned by Noel and Carson Hibbard.

mind that the UKCI is prepared and willing to work along with the National Rat Terrier Association in the promotion and administration of quality showing and breeding. Both of these organizations have adopted the same breed standard and share goals that include sacrificing in the market place in order to keep the breed pure.

Some of the following information on the Rat Terrier was supplied to the author from Mr. Dennis Eiland of Opp, Alabama. He has done extensive research on the Rat Terrier and is a regular columnist for Full Cry Magazine, a monthly publication devoted to hunting and treeing dogs.

CHARACTERISTICS OF THE RAT TERRIER

The Rat Terrier comes in three sizes: Toy, Mini, and Standard. The Toy Rat Terrier requires extreme selective breeding and weighs ten pounds or less. He is a dedicated dog, not as capable of hunting larger game as his bigger brothers and sisters, but quite able to catch rats and mice. His disposition makes him a wonderful companion. He, too, is endowed with all the traits of the larger-sized Rat Terriers.

The Mini Rat Terrier is produced by selective mating and weighs between 10 and 18 lbs. He is a capable hunter, a good treeing dog, and an exceptional pet.

The Standard (ratting or squirrel type) weighs between 18 and 28 lbs. He is a natural ratter and, at present, very popular in the southern United States. As a squirrel dog, this size Rat Terrier is most versatile. He is used for catching varmints and killing snakes, akunka, possum, and racoon. The standard Rat Terrier makes an excellent watchdog because of his intelligence and inborn desire to please his owner.

The Rat Terrier has proven himself to be a popular dog, both in Great Britain as well as in the United

Opposite: Trick or treat! The Rat Terrier's love for his owner is immeasurable and author Linda Hibbard and her Rat Terrier do everything together.

Endowed with all the traits of his larger cousins, the Toy Rat Terrier weighs under ten pounds and makes the perfect-sized companion. Pintica Baby, owned by Barbara Castro, is an adorable example.

States. His popularity can be traced to several factors: He is a small dog, short coated, easy to take care of, and genetically sound. The Rat Terrier has sound breeding qualities that give him the potential for a long life. It is not uncommon for this dog to live to be 18 or 19 years of age. He makes a fine pet, companion, and hunting dog. Rat Terriers are noted for their ability to hunt varmint and rid an infested area of rats and mice in a short period of time.

The Rat Terrier is an attractive dog and possesses great loyalty for his owner. The dog has a natural slick satin coat that is extremely easy to care for. The breed requires very little grooming and can survive in just about any climate, from extreme cold to hot temperatures. Rat Terriers make excellent indoor as well as outdoor pets.

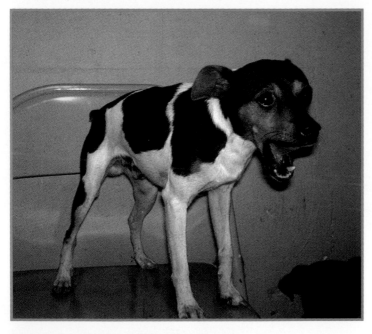

Possessing a great sense of humor, the playful Rat Terrier will do anything for a laugh. Pinto owned by Barbara Castro cracks himself up.

LIVING WITH A RAT TERRIER

Rosalie Ranear, a well-known breeder of Rat Terriers, tells us that "The Rat Terrier is the dog that everybody wants and few people know about." This statement couldn't be more true. These little dogs are so loved by their owners that most do not hesitate to relay stories about their little companions. One of my favorite stories is that about a farmer who had a little Rat Terrier. The dog gathered the eggs from the chicken coop every day for several years. The remarkable part about the story is that the dog never dropped an egg.

The small-sized but hardy Rat Terrier makes a great companion.

Rat Terriers are excellent companions for older people. As a small dog, it does not cost much to feed them. They are both obedient and loyal to their master. They do not require much space, and are clean and well-mannered. However, Rat Terriers by nature do need proper exercise and a prospective owner should be committed to seeing that the dog has adequate exercise and fresh air. A long brisk walk at least two or three times a week should suffice.

Rat Terriers are special dogs for those that love to hunt and are fine competition dogs. Rat Terriers are noted for their ability for treeing squirrels and make wonderful dogs for people who enjoy sporting raccoon and squirrel.

Rat Terriers are fine city dogs, too. They love to be with people and especially enjoy playing with children. The Rat Terrier is intelligent and loyal. These little dogs literally try to be part of your life. They provide unconditional love to their owners and all they ask in return is that you love them back.

Rat Terrier are fine hunting dogs and make great competitors. If you love the outdoors, this is the dog for you! Dennis Eiland and Stallion.

STANDARD FOR THE RAT TERRIER

The NRTA Rat Terrier Breed standard as written by the National Rat Terrier Association and adopted by the Universal Kennel Club International (UKCI) and the Rat Terrier Club of America.

Head:

Muzzle—Medium long, tapered but not snipy. Distance approximately equal to skull. Moderate stop. *Fault*: too sharp of a stop like seen in the Chihuahua breed.

Stop—Medium, tapered. Not sharp.

Skull—Slightly rounded. *Fault*: apple or dome head.

Nose—Black, slate, brown or shaded according with coat color. *Fault*: bulging eyes.

Bite—Level or Scissors. *Fault*: undershot or overshot.

Ears—Wedge-shaped, placed well up on side of head. Preferred erect. Semi-erect (tipped) and button

In the Rat Terrier, either ear carriage is considered correct. These two dogs show examples of both erect and semi-erect ear sets. This is Foxie Lady and Sorcerer owned by Margaret Burz.

The Rat Terrier can be seen in a variety of colors. Little Bit'A Ginger is a tan and white dog, while Fire Mountain Tuz is a tricolor. Owners, Jock and Susan Denney.

acceptable. *Fault*: spaced too far apart, one up and one down, round and bat-like.

Body—(Class A)-Height approximately the same length. Length not to exceed one and one-half inches from height. (Class B)-for the short leg type, body length not to exceed three inches in proportion to length. *Fault:* excessive barrel chest or round body.

Neck—Moderately long, strong, giving good support to head.

Shoulders—Sloping and well arched.

Back—Straight and strong. *Fault*: roached, sway or rounded rump.

Tail—Carried erect, set high. When docked as a puppy leave approximately three quarters of an inch on the dog. When docked as adults leave approximately two to two and one-half inches on the dog. *Fault*: full tail or no tail unless born a natural bob.

Back Legs—Strong in thigh, slight angulation in hock. Stifle neither turned in nor out. *Fault*: cow hocked or bowed.

Tuck-up—Slight.

Elbows—Held close and perpendicular to the body. *Fault*: turned in or out. Bow legs.

Chest—Fairly deep, well ribbed. *Fault*: too narrow or excessively barrel chested.

Coat—Short, smooth, shiny. *Fault*: too thin.

Colors—Black, blue, red, lemon, charcoal, or liver. Browns (sable, fawn, tan). Chocolate and liver must have chocolate, liver or red nose.

Even as a puppy, the Rat Terrier should retain his true terrier heritage while demonstrating good temperament and a friendly demeanor.

Markings—with white, with tan, with white and tan.

Patterns—Tri, piebald (patches of color), solid, brindle (on face only).

Weight—Toy-10 lbs or less, Mini-over 10 lbs but under 18 lbs, Standard-over 18 lbs but not exceeding 28 lbs.

Movement—Smooth flowing legs moving straight, agile.

Character—Pleasant, easy to get along with, quick, alert, agile, fleet. Retaining his true terrier heritage by being a superb ratter and worker. While active outdoors, he makes a wonderful house pet, companion, and watchdog. At ease at home relaxing with his master doing well with the family. Hardy enough to withstand a child's roughest play.

Please note: Class A is of the longer-legged squarer type. Class B is of the shorter-legged stockier type. Both can be shown in the appropriate classes. All other standards will apply to both types.

Disqualifications—Dogs that cannot be brought under control. Monorchid and Cryptorchid. Pure white and merle color. Brindle on body other than face.

Fault means that points will be taken off a particular trait, it does not mean the dog cannot compete. Disqualification means that the dog cannot compete in an official show.

SELECTING YOUR RAT TERRIER

After you and your family have familiarized yourselves with the nature of the Rat Terrier and feel committed to owning one of your own, it is now time to find a suitable dog. Remember, you will be planning for the life of a new family member and friend for many years to come.

It is a good idea to decide if you feel more comfortable about adopting an older dog or a new puppy. When making your decision, keep in mind that an adult dog has a past and has been reared in his formative years by another person. If you know the individual that has raised the dog, then you can easily familiarize yourself with the animal's personality. In any case, it's a good idea to try to find out something about the dog's past life. This will enable you to determine if his personality traits will fit in with your family.

A basketful of love and surprises await you if you decide to bring a Rat Terrier into your home.

An older dog can make a fine pet for an older person. He may possess characteristics that make for a good breeding animal or an excellent hunter. Check to see if the dog has been used to staying outdoors, and if he has, you should either keep him for a yard dog or try to domesticate him.

Choosing a puppy is an adventure. It is always exciting and pleasurable to see newborn puppies running and playing. Selecting your new puppy from a whole litter affords you many opportunities. You will be able to observe how the puppy interacts with his littermates. Pay close attention to all the puppies and observe how they interact with one another. Dominance within the litter has much to say about how your puppy will behave later in life. Each litter has its own personality. Some litters are

more docile while others tend to be much more inquisitive. The traits within a litter should indicate to you what type of dog you will be getting. If you are interested in a pet that will be your constant companion, it might be wise to choose a more tranquil puppy. If you desire a hunting and treeing dog, then you should select a puppy that tends to be larger and more aggressive in nature.

The puppy you choose will be a family member for a long time, so pick the healthiest puppy available.

Give careful consideration to the sex of the perspective pet. Some people are naturally more partial to the female, while others may wish to own a male. Female dogs will come into season twice a year, and during this time she is capable of having puppies. If you don't intend to breed quality Rat Terriers, it is imperative to have your dog spayed or neutered. This will make for a better pet and help to prevent them

Observing the way a puppy interacts with his littermates can tell you a lot about his personality.

from developing certain types of cancers associated with the reproductive system.

Puppies are always cute and cuddly, and Rat Terrier pups are adorable. They are simplistic in their appearance and yet portray the regal qualities of the sophisticated animal they will grow into—just about everybody is drawn to them. The Rat Terrier is a most desirable little dog. He is lively, spirited, full of energy, and terribly curious about his world. The Rat Terrier has large, shoe-button brown eyes that look sweet and gentle. He looks like he wouldn't get into any trouble, but anybody who has ever owned one of these little bundles of energy can easily tell you he will need constant supervision and guidance. Remember the breed's unspoken motto: "How can I please my master?" He dearly wants to please his owner, but like all living things, he needs guidance and direction. Without adequate supervision, it would not be uncommon to find that he has gotten into the bathroom, discovered the roll of toilet paper and strung it throughout the house. He, of course, will be most careful not to stop his activity until every sheet of toilet tissue is off the roll. Care has to be taken to prevent unwanted work. If you prefer a small pet that will be your constant companion, a Toy might be the type best suited to your needs. Rat Terriers are quite versatile animals. They make excellent hunters, companions and all-around good guard dogs.

The pup you choose will have a better start in life if both his parents are healthy and well adjusted. Janice owned by Ralph Jackson plays with her puppies.

Color can be an important consideration if you intend to breed your dogs. Should you be interested in the traditional tricolored dog of black, white, and tans, or the more exotic colors such as blue or chocolate, you can place your order with a breeder for your specific choices.

Our population of dogs is excessive and we must bear in mind that not all people are responsible owners. All too often we hear of people taking home an adorable little puppy only to find that the dog did not fit into their family. Tragically, the unwanted animal can end up at an overcrowded shelter. Be a responsible pet owner. Learn about the nature and character of the Rat Terrier, be deliberate in your purchase, and select your dog from a reputable breeder. Remember the Rat Terrier is a rare breed!

WHERE TO BUY YOUR RAT TERRIER

Where should you look for a quality Rat Terrier? There are pet stores, advertisements in local newspapers, and ads on the World Wide Web. These choices are limited to stock on hand. Without a doubt, the best place to purchase a good Rat Terrier is through a breeder. You can obtain a list of quality breeders from the Universal Kennel Club International (UKCI) for a minimal fee. There are primarily two kinds of breeders: the professional and the hobbyist. The professional breeder is one that has studied the breed standard and constantly tries to produce dogs of top quality. Most often, a professional breeder is not in business just for money. They are individuals that care for their animals and care about the future of the breed. A quality breeder is not limited in stock. It would not be uncommon for a good breeder to have several females that have litters and others that will be bred in the near future. This gives the prospective buyer the choice of size, color, and disposition. A good breeder will take orders for puppies even before they are born.

Hobbyist breeders are people who are raising dogs as a hobby or for part-time income. Be careful when purchasing from a casual breeder and make certain that the seller knows something about the breed standard. Inquire if the puppies have been inoculated and wormed. Most importantly, make sure you get a written guarantee that if the puppy has a congenital disorder or becomes ill shortly after purchase, you can get your money back. Long-established breeders will guarantee your dog is free from congenital health defects and in good health at the time of the purchase.

When looking for a breed as rare as the Rat Terrier, it is not likely that you will find advertisements in your local newspaper. The World Wide Web can be a viable source of information when making a purchase. Should you make connections with a breeder that seems interesting, question to see if he is a member of the National Rat Terrier Association or the Rat Terrier Club of America. This should give you a clue as to whether the breeding was done with knowl-

A responsible breeder will have started the socialization process before you take your puppy home. A well-socialized Rat Terrier will get along with anyone! Carson Hibbard with Bridget, a tri-colored Rat Terrier.

edge of the breed standard. If the seller seems put out, or does not want to answer your questions, chances are he is not the right person for you.

The most credible source of finding a good Rat Terrier is from a long-established breeder. There are a number of such businesses that have studied the genetic breeding and have been producing Rat Terriers of quality for many years. Their knowledge is extensive, and their kennels are known throughout the United States. One example, Bab's Farm in Homestead, Florida, is owned and operated by Barbara Castro. Ms. Castro has been breeding fine Rat Terriers for years and has also been instrumental in writing the standard for the breed. She is a member of the National Rat Terrier Association.

In Button Willow, California, Ms. Rosalie Rinear has been breeding Rat Terriers for many years. Her kennel, Fire Mountain Rat Terriers, is known for its quality breeding. Fire Mountain Rat Terriers are highly papered and carry a health guarantee. Ms. Rinear was also instrumental in writing the breed standard. She is a member of the National Rat Terrier Club of America and has spent much of her life working for the promotion and betterment of the breed. Her kennel and her dogs are popular throughout the United States.

A pup's personality will be evident in the way he interacts with his littermates. It's not hard to see who is top dog around here!

Bridget, owned by Nolan and Linda Hibbard, was bred by Rosalie Rinear.

The Rat Terrier is a rare breed, but perhaps the rarest of the breed is the Decker Giants. They originated in Alvadore, Oregon, and were bred by Milton Decker. He raised the largest of the Rat Terriers that ranged in size from 29 to over 45 pounds. He raised quality dogs that were excellent hunters not only of varmints, but also outstanding hunters of deer and game birds.

Although the Deckers are no longer raising their Giant Rat Terriers, Ms. Rosalie Rinear continues to raise these fine hunting and companion dogs. They are registered through the Universal Kennel Club International and possess the same colors and standards as the smaller, more popular Rat Terriers. The National Rat Terrier Association recognizes the Decker Giants and finds them to be dogs of superior intelligence and devotion to their owners.

CARING FOR THE RAT TERRIER

The Rat Terrier doesn't need to go to high-priced dog salons for his grooming needs. Because they are short-coated and hearty dogs, the care of their skin and coat is minimal. There are certain supplies, however, that are necessary for properly grooming your dog. A fine-tooth flea comb, a medium bristle brush, and a pair of good quality nail clippers are basic supplies that every dog owner should purchase.

Before you start to brush your dog, it is advisable to comb through the coat with a flea comb, taking care to check for flea eggs, live fleas, or other parasites that might be present on the dog's skin. When eggs or parasites are visible, immediately treat the infestation by using a flea spray or medicated shampoo to

Due to his short coat, the Rat Terrier is a low-maintenance dog in terms of his grooming requirements.

Regular check-ups are an important part of your Rat Terrier's health and help maintain his quality of life. Dr. Mel White with a medium-sized Rat Terrier.

prevent the spread of further contamination to the skin. Your local pet store will have products that have proven to be quite effective in preventing unwanted hosts on the dog for at least four weeks.

After making sure the dog's skin is free from parasites, give you Rat Terrier's coat a good five minute brushing each day. Brushing the dog's coat keeps his fur free from dustmites, dandruff, and loose hair; it also prevents itching that will result in biting and scratching of skin.

Rat Terriers should be bathed every one to three months, depending on their lifestyle. A dog that spends a good deal of time indoors should not need to be bathed as often. Bathing your dog too frequently can

If you accustom your Rat Terrier to grooming procedures when he is young, he will come to think of it as a pleasant experience.

cause the coat to lose natural luster and sheen. Take care that when you do give your dog a bath, you remove all soap from the skin. If you do not, your dog will surely develop dandruff or skin irritation.

CARE OF THE TOENAILS

Rat Terriers need to have their toenails trimmed frequently, especially if they spend most of their time indoors. Running on pavement or gravel tends to keep the nails worn down. Not keeping nails properly groomed can result in damage to the feet and possible lameness.

Purchase a pair of good quality nail clippers. Cutting your dog's nails is not a difficult procedure. Hold the Rat Terrier firmly and look closely at the dog's nails. If the toenails are white or pink, you can easily see the blood vessels and most importantly, the quick of the nail. Make sure that you do not cut or nick the vessel. If you cut too closely to the quick and hit the live part of the nail, the dog most likely will become frightened and his nail will bleed. If an accident should occur, wipe the nail with a cotton-tipped swab dipped in rubbing alcohol or hydrogen peroxide. If bleeding continues, put a piece of cotton next to the nail and apply gentle pressure.

An easy, safe, and inexpensive way to care for your dog's nails is to purchase a power buffer to shape and trim the nails. You can also go to most pet shops that groom dogs and have the nails groomed with the nail buffer for a nominal amount of money. Rat Terriers tend to have sensitive feet because they use their paws for digging. Periodically check the pads of the feet for cracks in the skin. If you see open cracks, apply petroleum jelly to the area. After you have finished grooming the

A Rat Terrier's feet must be inspected regularly and his toenails kept short to prevent any tearing or discomfort.

nails and the pads of the feet, be sure to reward your dog with a treat, a hug, and a kiss.

DENTAL HYGIENE

While the Rat Terrier is still a puppy, it is wise to purchase a dog toothbrush and a tube of enzymatic toothpaste. These items can be purchased at any major pet store. Get your dog used to having his teeth brushed. The 2-Brush™ by Nylabone® is designed to brush both sides of your dog's teeth at the same time. Each brush contains dog-designed toothpaste that your Rat Terrier will love. Rat Terriers have a long life span and it is not at all unusual for small, active, long-lived dogs to suffer from dental tartar buildup and

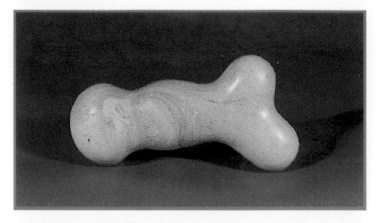

The Galileo™ is the toughest dog bone ever made. It is flavored to appeal to your Rat Terrier and annealed so it has a relatively soft outer layer. It is a necessary chew device and Rat Terrier pacifier.

eventually cavities. These conditions, if not averted, will result in loss of teeth as your dog ages.

Nylabone® products such as Roar-Hide™ bones, CarrotBones™ and POPpups™ all help to remove tartar from the teeth. Rat Terriers love to have something to chew on, especially when they are bored. You will find it also cuts down on eating for the sake of eating. Some dogs, much like people, have a need to chew or have something in their mouths all the time.

Your veterinarian should examine your dog's teeth on a regular basis. These examinations are part of your dog's preventative care.

CARE OF YOUR DOG'S EARS

It is necessary that the dog's ears be examined periodically and cleaned when necessary. Should

A thorough oral examination should be a part of your Rat Terrier's grooming routine.

wax or dirt build up inside the ears, a cotton-tipped swab dipped in alcohol should be inserted inside the folds of the outer ear. Cleaning is not difficult. If you are taking care of an active puppy, it is advisable to have one person hold the dog firmly while the other cleans the ears. Take care not to insert the cotton swab too deeply into the ear canal as this could damage the ear drum. Cleaning the ears prevents ear mites and other problems caused by poor hygiene.

EXERCISING YOUR RAT TERRIER

Exercise is a must for the Rat Terrier. He not only likes to run and play, it seems to be essential to the dog's very nature. Rat Terriers were bred for hunting.

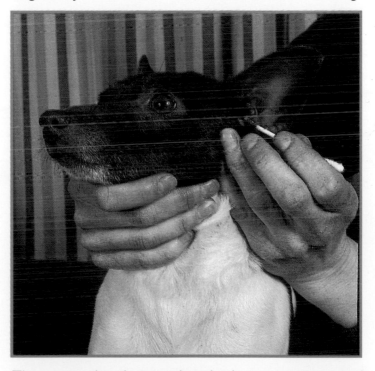

Your Rat Terrier's ears should be kept clean and free of waxy build-up.

They are a dog that needs to be in open spaces and smell grass, trees, and flowers. Rat Terriers need to run and exercise their muscles.

The Rat Terrier is most adaptable and will adjust just fine to an apartment or small house. However, it will be necessary that your dog go on long walks every day. The Rat Terrier is happy no matter where he lives as long as he is treated well and his basic needs are met. His aim in life is to please his master; he is a very loving and affectionate dog.

Rat Terriers must be supervised in their daily exercise. They seem to get confused when allowed to run loose on busy streets. If you allow your dog to do this, you run the risk that a car could hit the dog and seriously injure or kill him. Rat Terriers are inclined to lose their lives prematurely to larger dogs that overtake them in dog fights. Proper care should be taken that when your dog is not indoors he is contained in a fenced yard or walked on a leash.

TRAINING THE RAT TERRIER

It is always a good idea to take any dog to obedience training. It helps the animal to learn what is expected of him. The Rat Terrier loves to be in the limelight. He adores being the center of attention. This, coupled with his high degree of intelligence, makes it extremely easy to train him.

A well-trained and well-groomed Rat Terrier is a joy to own.

For the most part, housebreaking a new puppy is a very easy task. Spread newspaper over the area where you want your puppy to go. When he starts to turn in circles or sniff an area of the house, put him on his papers. When he is finished, praise him. You will be surprised to learn how quickly your new puppy will respond. After he has mastered paper training, it is a good time to get him used to going outside. When he is outside relate a familiar word or two to him that he can associate with his paper training. Rat Terriers are remarkably smart and it can't be stressed enough their eagerness to please their owners.

HUNTING WITH THE RAT TERRIER

The traditional sport of hunting with the Rat Terrier still continues today. Matthew Hinson and Josh Hall with Magic and Stallion show off the fruits of their labor.

The Rat Terrier has a genetic proclivity for hunting. So deeply ingrained in his nature is the desire to hunt that his second name is the "squirrel dog." He loves to hunt pig, raccoon, squirrel, rats, and mice.

For us to fully understand the Rat Terrier's inclination and need to hunt requires that we go back to the dog's ancestry and genetic make-up. Much of our own hunting heritage comes from English settlers on the frontier.

Dennis Eiland, writer for *Full Cry Magazine* and a breeder and researcher of the Rat Terrier explains, "Most of us are familiar with the sport of fox hunting, English style. The very thought of it brings to mind English noblemen riding horses and attired in red

The instinct to chase small game is ingrained in the Rat Terrier's nature. Stallion treeing on a squirrel.

coats and black leather boots. The hunting cry of 'Tally Ho' could be heard as a pack of foxhounds began pursuit of a wily red fox. Best known was the use of the Fox Terrier to flush the quarry from its den once the hounds ran to the ground."

Fox Terriers, ancestors of the Rat Terrier, were highly prized by the English. The breed had few if any genetic faults. The dog was hardy and easy to care for. The Fox Terrier would not back down to his game—making him quite popular with the huntsman of the time. The dogs were always lively, agile, good-tempered, and most of all, dedicated to pleasing their masters. The little dogs wrapped themselves around their master's hearts and became part of their lives. The Fox Terrier, although bonded to the huntsman, was also adaptive and eager to be part of the family. The breed loved to play children's games with their young owners. These traits, combined with their sophisticated and regal look, were most appealing to both nobility and commoners alike.

The Manchester Terrier also existed in England in the 1820s. The breed was popular, but not as well known as the Fox Terrier. The Manchester was also known for his keen ability to hunt and to keep down the rodent population. The English hunted the Manchester along the marshes and canals in pursuit of "reed rats." These rats were large, vicious rodents, some weighing up to 17 pounds and possessed teeth that resembled small daggers. The reed rat was a formidable foe for any dog and the Manchester Terrier didn't have any difficulty seeking out and destroying his prey.

Both the Fox and the Manchester Terriers in the 1820s were quite different dogs from the ones that exist today. Both dogs were extremely muscular and their skin was as tough as a piece of tanned hide. The Fox Terrier was known as being the more versatile of the two terriers. He proved himself to be a proficient hunter and yet an excellent pet—qualities making for a close relationship between the dog and his master.

The Rat Terrier is trained to pick up the scent of the game before he ever begins to hunt. Smokey and Magic, owned by Dennis Eiland, get used to the smell and presence of this squirrel, who is safe in his cage.

YOUR PUPPY'S NEW HOME

Before actually collecting your puppy, it is better that you purchase the basic items you will need in advance of the pup's arrival date. This allows you more opportunity to shop around and ensure you have exactly what you want rather than having to buy lesser quality in a hurry.

It is always better to collect the puppy as early in the day as possible. In most instances this will mean that the puppy has a few hours with your family before it is time to retire for his first night's sleep away from his former home.

If the breeder is local, then you may not need any form of box to place the puppy in when you bring him home. A member of the family can hold the pup in his lap—duly protected by some towels just in case the

Opposite: It is easy to fall in love with the cute and affectionate Rat Terrier, but make sure the decision to buy one is considered carefully. Margaret Burz with her dogs Ohtow and Moon.

Below: Before you put him in the car and take him home, be sure your household and your family is prepared for the arrival of your new Rat Terrier.

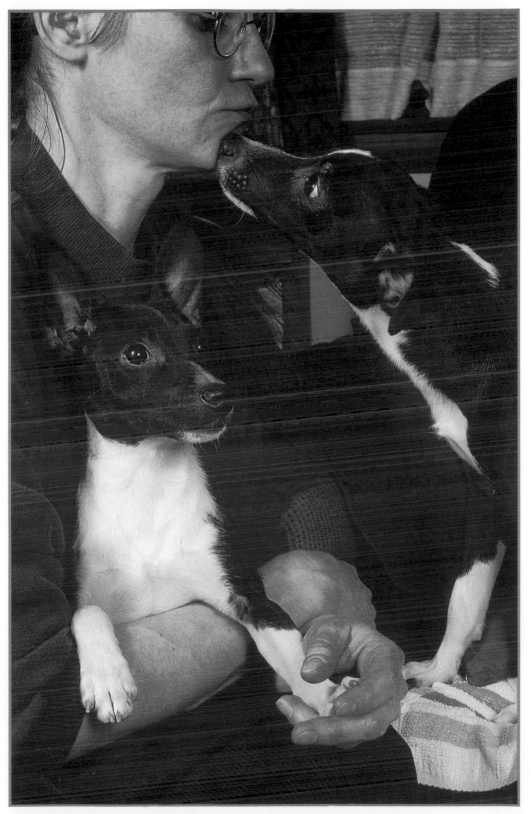

puppy becomes car sick! Be sure to advise the breeder at what time you hope to arrive for the puppy, as this will obviously influence the feeding of the pup that morning or afternoon. If you arrive early in the day, then they will likely only give the pup a light breakfast so as to reduce the risk of travel sickness.

If the trip will be of a few hours duration, you should take a travel crate with you. The crate will provide your pup with a safe place to lie down and rest during the trip. During the trip, the puppy will no doubt wish to relieve his bowels, so you will have to make a few stops. On a long journey you may need a rest yourself, and can take the opportunity to let the puppy get some fresh air. However, do not let the puppy walk where

When deciding on a puppy, check to see if the breeder runs a quality facility and all the dogs are clean, healthy, and well taken care of.

there may have been a lot of other dogs because he might pick up an infection. Also, if he relieves his bowels at such a time, do not just leave the feces where they were dropped. This is the height of irre-sponsibility. It has resulted in many public parks and other places actually banning dogs. You can pur-chase poop-scoops from your pet shop and should have them with you whenever you are taking the dog out where he might foul a public place.

Your journey home should be made as quickly as possible. If it is a hot day, be sure the car interior is amply supplied with fresh air. It should never be too hot or too cold for the puppy. The pup must never be placed where he might be subject to a draft. If the journey requires an overnight stop at a motel, be aware that other guests will not appreciate a puppy crying half the night. You must regard the puppy as a baby and comfort him so he does not cry for long periods. The worst thing you can do is to shout at or smack him. This will mean your relationship is off to a

Provide your Rat Terrier with a crate of his own. He will soon come to think of it as a cozy den in which to retreat and relax.

really bad start. You wouldn't smack a baby, and your puppy is still very much just this.

ON ARRIVING HOME

By the time you arrive home the puppy may be very tired, in which case he should be taken to his sleeping area and allowed to rest. Children should not be allowed to interfere with the pup when he is sleeping. If the pup is not tired, he can be allowed to investigate his new home—but always under your close supervision. After a short look around, the puppy will no doubt appreciate a light meal and a drink of water. Do not overfeed him at his first meal because he will be in an excited state and more likely to be sick.

Although it is an obvious temptation, you should not invite friends and neighbors around to see the new arrival until he has had at least 48 hours in which to settle down. Indeed, if you can delay this longer then do so, especially if the puppy is not fully vaccinated. At the very least, the visitors might introduce some local bacteria on their clothing that the puppy is not immune to. This aspect is always a risk when a pup has been moved some distance, so the fewer people the pup meets in the first week or so the better.

DANGERS IN THE HOME

Your home holds many potential dangers for a little mischievous puppy, so you must think about these in advance and be sure he is protected from them. The more obvious are as follows:

Open Fires. All open fires should be protected by a mesh screen guard so there is no danger of the pup being burned by spitting pieces of coal or wood.

Electrical Wires. Puppies just love chewing on things, so be sure that all electrical appliances are neatly hidden from view and are not left plugged in when not in use. It is not sufficient simply to turn the plug switch to the off position—pull the plug from the socket.

Open Doors. A door would seem a pretty innocuous object, yet with a strong draft it could kill or injure a puppy easily if it is slammed shut. Always ensure there is no risk of this happening. It is most likely during warm weather when you have windows or outside doors open and a sudden gust of wind blows through.

Balconies. If you live in a high-rise building, obviously the pup must be protected from falling. Be sure he cannot get through any railings on your patio, balcony, or deck.

The great outdoors can hold many dangers for your Rat Terrier puppy, so closely supervise him when he is outside. Phoebie, owned by Nolan Hibbard.

Puppies love to chew on things, so make sure that all electrical appliances are neatly hidden from view and unplugged when not in use.

Ponds and Pools. A garden pond or a swimming pool is a very dangerous place for a little puppy to be near. Be sure it is well screened so there is no risk of the pup falling in. It takes barely a minute for a pup—or a child—to drown.

The Kitchen. While many puppies will be kept in the kitchen, at least while they are toddlers and not able to control their bowel movements, this is a room full of danger—especially while you are cooking. When cooking, keep the puppy in a play pen or in another room where he is safely out of harm's way. Alternatively, if you have a carry box or crate, put him in this so he can still see you but is well protected.

Be aware, when using washing machines, that more than one puppy has clambered in and decided to have a nap and received a wash instead! If you leave the washing machine door open and leave the room for any reason, then be sure to check inside the machine before you close the door and switch on.

Small Children. Toddlers and small children should never be left unsupervised with puppies. In spite of such advice it is amazing just how many people not only do this but also allow children to pull and maul pups. They should be taught from the outset that a puppy is not a plaything to be dragged about the home—and they should be promptly scolded if they disobey.

51

Make sure your Rat Terrier is always in a secure fenced-in area when off lead. This is Nic and Penney pure Decker Giants, owned by Tim Brown.

Children must be shown how to lift a puppy so it is safe. Failure by you to correctly educate your children about dogs could one day result in their getting a very nasty bite or scratch. When a puppy is lifted, his weight must always be supported. To lift the pup, first place your right hand under his chest. Next, secure the pup by using your left hand to hold his neck. Now you can lift him and bring him close to your chest. Never lift a pup by his ears and, while he can be lifted by the scruff of his neck where the fur is loose, there is no reason ever to do this, so don't.

Beyond the dangers already cited you may be able to think of other ones that are specific to your home—

Give your Rat Terrier plenty of safe chew toys like Nylabones® to keep his teeth happy and away from your valuables.

steep basement steps or the like. Go around your home and check out all potential problems—you'll be glad you did.

THE FIRST NIGHT

The first few nights a puppy spends away from his mother and littermates are quite traumatic for him. He will feel very lonely, maybe cold, and will certainly miss the heartbeat of his siblings when sleeping. To help overcome his loneliness it may help to place a clock next to his bed—one with a loud tick. This will in some way soothe him, as the clock ticks to a rhythm

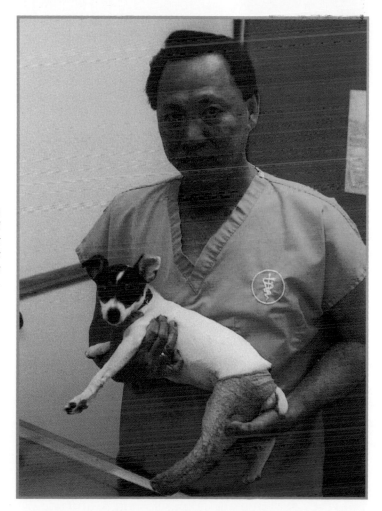

A good relationship with your veterinarian will ensure that your Rat Terrier receives the best care. Dr. Brian Tan treats Vickie for a broken leg.

not dissimilar from a heart beat. A cuddly toy may also help in the first few weeks. A dim nightlight may provide some comfort to the puppy, because his eyes will not yet be fully able to see in the dark. The puppy may want to leave his bed for a drink or to relieve himself.

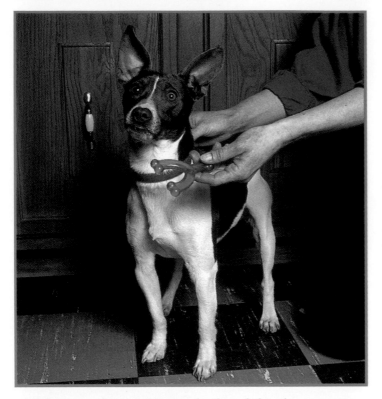

Rat Terriers love to chew, so give him plenty of Nylabones® to keep him occupied while exercising his teeth and gums. Phantom owned by Chet Jackson.

If the pup does whimper in the night, there are two things you should not do. One is to get up and chastise him, because he will not understand why you are shouting at him; and the other is to rush to comfort him every time he cries because he will quickly realize that if he wants you to come running all he needs to do is to holler loud enough!

By all means give your puppy some extra attention on his first night, but after this quickly refrain from so doing. The pup will cry for a while but then settle down and go to sleep. Some pups are, of course, worse than others in this respect, so you must use balanced judgment in the matter. Many owners take their pups to bed with them, and there is certainly nothing wrong with this.

The pup will be no trouble in such cases. However, you should only do this if you intend to let this be a permanent arrangement, otherwise it is hardly fair to the puppy. If you have decided to have two puppies, then they will keep each other company and you will have few problems.

OTHER PETS

If you have other pets in the home then the puppy must be introduced to them under careful supervision. Puppies will get on just fine with any other pets—but you must make due allowance for the respective sizes of the pets concerned, and appreciate that your puppy has a rather playful nature. It would be very foolish to leave him with a young rabbit. The pup will want to play and might bite the bunny and get altogether too rough with it. Kittens are more able to defend themselves from overly cheeky pups, who will get a quick scratch if they overstep the mark. The adult cat could obviously give the pup a very bad scratch, though generally cats will jump clear of pups and watch them from a suitable vantage point. Eventually they will meet at ground level where the cat will quickly hiss and box a puppy's ears. The pup will soon learn to respect an adult cat; thereafter they will probably develop into great friends as the pup matures into an adult dog.

HOUSETRAINING

Undoubtedly, the first form of training your puppy will undergo is in respect to his toilet habits. To achieve this you can use either newspaper, or a large

Your new Rat Terrier may miss the company of his dam and littermates, so shower extra attention on him when you first bring him to his new home.

litter tray filled with soil or lined with newspaper. A puppy cannot control his bowels until he is a few months old, and not fully until he is an adult. Therefore you must anticipate his needs and be prepared for a few accidents. The prime times a pup will urinate and defecate are shortly after he wakes up from a sleep, shortly after he has eaten, and after he has been playing awhile. He will usually whimper and start searching the room for a suitable place. You must quickly pick him up and place him on the newspaper or in the litter tray. Hold him in position gently but firmly. He might jump out of the box without doing anything on the first one or two occasions, but if you simply repeat the procedure every time you think he wants to relieve himself then eventually he will get the message.

When he does defecate as required, give him plenty of praise, telling him what a good puppy he is. The litter tray or newspaper must, of course, be cleaned or replaced after each use—puppies do not like using a dirty toilet any more than you do. The pup's toilet can be placed near the kitchen door and as he gets older the tray can be placed outside while the door is open. The pup will then start to use it while he is outside. From that time on, it is easy to get the pup to use a given area of the yard.

Many breeders recommend the popular alternative of crate training. Upon bringing the pup home, introduce him to his crate. The open wire crate is the best choice, placed in a restricted, draft-free area of the home. Put the pup's Nylabone® and other favorite toys in the crate along with a wool blanket or other suitable bedding. The puppy's natural cleanliness instincts prohibit him from soiling in the place where he sleeps, his crate. The puppy should be allowed to go in and out of the open crate during the day, but he should sleep in the crate at the night and at other intervals during the day. Whenever the pup is taken out of his crate, he should be brought outside (or to his newspapers) to do his business. Never use the crate as a place of punishment. You will see how quickly your pup takes to his crate, considering it as his own safe haven from the big world around him.

THE EARLY DAYS

You will no doubt be given much advice on how to bring up your puppy. This will come from dog-owning friends, neighbors, and through articles and books you may read on the subject. Some of the advice will

Your Rat Terrier will need your love, discipline, and guidance in order to become a valued family member and companion.

be sound, some will be nothing short of rubbish. What you should do above all else is to keep an open mind and let common sense prevail over prejudice and worn-out ideas that have been handed down over the centuries. There is no one way that is superior to all others, no more than there is no one dog that is exactly a replica of another. Each is an individual and must always be regarded as such.

A dog never becomes disobedient, unruly, or a menace to society without the full consent of his owner. Your puppy may have many limitations, but the singular biggest limitation he is confronted with in so many instances is his owner's inability to understand his needs and how to cope with them.

IDENTIFICATION

It is a sad reflection on our society that the number of dogs and cats stolen every year runs into many thousands. To these can be added the number that get lost. If you do not want your cherished pet to be lost or stolen, then you should see that he is carrying a permanent identification number, as well as a temporary tag on his collar.

Permanent markings come in the form of tattoos placed either inside the pup's ear flap, or on the inner side of a pup's upper rear leg. The number given is then recorded with one of the national registration companies. Research laboratories will not purchase dogs carrying numbers as they realize these are clearly someone's pet, and not abandoned animals. As a result, thieves will normally abandon dogs so marked and this at least gives the dog a chance to be taken to the police or the dog pound, when the number can be traced and the dog reunited with its family. The only problem with this method at this time is that there are a number of registration bodies, so it is not always apparent which one the dog is registered with (as you provide the actual number). However, each registration body is aware of his competitors and will normally be happy to supply their addresses. Those holding the dog can check out which one you are with. It is not a perfect system, but until such is developed it's the best available.

Another permanent form of identification is the microchip, a computer chip that is no bigger than a grain of rice, that is injected between the dog's shoulder blades. The dog feels no discomfort. The dog also recieves a tag that says he is microchipped. If the dog is lost and picked up by the humane society, they can trace the owner by scanning the microchip. It is the safest form of identification.

A temporary tag takes the form of a metal or plastic disk large enough for you to place the dog's name and your phone number on it—maybe even your address as well. In virtually all places you will be required to obtain a license for your puppy. This may not become applicable until the pup is six months old, but it might apply regardless of his age. Much depends upon the state within a country, or the country itself, so check with your veterinarian if the breeder has not already advised you on this.

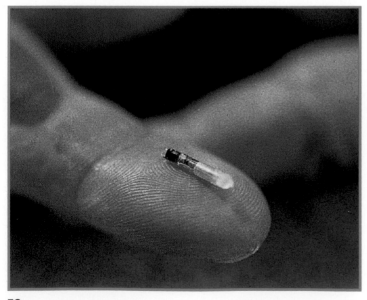

The newest method of identification is the microchip, a computer chip that is no bigger than a grain of rice that is injected into the dog's skin.

FEEDING YOUR RAT TERRIER

Dog owners today are fortunate in that they live in an age when considerable cash has been invested in the study of canine nutritional requirements. This means dog food manufacturers are very concerned about ensuring that their foods are of the best quality. The result of all of their studies, apart from the food itself, is that dog owners are bombarded with advertisements telling them why they must purchase a given brand. The number of products avail-

Show your Rat Terrier that you care by providing him with a high-quality dog food formulated for his stage of life and activity level.

able to you is unlimited, so it is hardly surprising to find that dogs in general suffer from obesity and an excess of vitamins, rather than the reverse. Be sure to feed age-appropriate food—puppy food up to one year of age, adult food thereafter. Generally breeders recommend dry food supplemented by canned, if needed.

FACTORS AFFECTING NUTRITIONAL NEEDS
Activity Level. A dog that lives in a country environment and is able to exercise for long periods of the

day will need more food than the same breed of dog living in an apartment and given little exercise.

Quality of the Food. Obviously the quality of food will affect the quantity required by a puppy. If the nutritional content of a food is low then the puppy will need more of it than if a better quality food was fed.

Balance of Nutrients and Vitamins. Feeding a puppy the correct balance of nutrients is not easy because the average person is not able to measure out ratios of one to another, so it is a case of trying to see that nothing is in excess. However, only tests, or your veterinarian, can be the source of reliable advice.

Genetic and Biological Variation. Apart from all of the other considerations, it should be remembered that each puppy is an individual. His genetic make-up will influence not only his physical characteristics but also his metabolic efficiency. This being so, two pups from the same litter can vary quite a bit in the amount of food they need to perform the same function under the same conditions. If you consider the potential combinations of all of these factors then you will see that pups of a given breed could vary quite a bit in the amount of food they will need. Before discussing feeding quantities it is valuable to know at least a little about the composition of food and its role in the body.

The POPpup™ is a healthy treat for your Rat Terrier. Its bone-hard structure helps control plaque and when microwaved, becomes a rich cracker that Rat Terriers love. It is available in different flavors and is fortified with calcium.

COMPOSITION AND ROLE OF FOOD

The main ingredients of food are protein, fats, and carbohydrates, each of which is needed in relatively large quantities when compared to the other needs of vitamins and minerals. The other vital ingredient of food is, of course, water. Although all foods obviously contain some of the basic ingredients needed for an animal to survive, they do not all contain the ingredients in the needed ratios or type. For example, there are many forms of protein, just as there are many types of carbohydrates. Both of these compounds are found in meat and in vegetable matter—but not all of those that are needed will be in one particular meat or vegetable. Plants, especially, do not contain certain amino acids that are required for the synthesis of certain proteins needed by dogs.

Likewise, vitamins are found in meats and vegetable matter, but vegetables are a richer source of most. Meat contains very little carbohydrates. Some vitamins can be synthesized by the dog, so do not need to be supplied via the food. Dogs are carnivores and this means their digestive tract has evolved to need a high quantity of meat as compared to humans. The digestive system of carnivores is unable to break down the tough cellulose walls of plant matter, but it is easily able to assimilate proteins from meat.

In order to gain its needed vegetable matter in a form that it can cope with, the carnivore eats all of its prey. This includes the partly digested food

Your Rat Terrier should have clean cool water available to him at all times.

within the stomach. In commercially prepared foods, the cellulose is broken down by cooking. During this process the vitamin content is either greatly reduced or lost altogether. The manufacturer therefore adds vitamins once the heat process has been completed. This is why commercial foods are so useful as part of a feeding regimen, providing they are of good quality and from a company that has prepared the foods very carefully.

Proteins

These are made from amino acids, of which at least ten are essential if a puppy is to maintain healthy growth. Proteins provide the building blocks for the puppy's body. The richest sources are meat, fish and poultry, together with their by-products. The latter will include milk, cheese, yogurt, fishmeal, and eggs. Vegetable matter that has a high protein content includes soy beans, together with numerous corn and other plant extracts that have been dehydrated. The actual protein content needed in the diet will be determined both by the activity level of the dog and his age. The total protein need will also be influenced by the digestibility factor of the food given.

Fats

These serve numerous roles in the puppy's body. They provide insulation against the cold, and help buffer the organs from knocks and general activity shocks. They provide the richest source of energy, and reserves of this, and they are vital in the transport of vitamins and other nutrients, via the blood, to all other organs. Finally, it is the fat content within a diet that gives it palatability. It is important that the fat content of a diet should not be excessive. This is because the high energy content of fats (more than twice that of protein or carbohydrate) will increase the overall energy content of the diet. The puppy will adjust its food intake to that of its energy needs, which are obviously more easily met in a high-energy diet. This will mean that while the fats are providing the energy needs of the puppy, the overall diet may not be providing its protein, vitamin, and mineral needs, so signs of protein deficiency will become apparent. Rich sources of fats are meat, their byproducts (butter, milk), and vegetable oils, such as safflower, olive, corn or soy bean.

Carbohydrates

These are the principal energy compounds given to puppies and adult dogs. Their inclusion within most commercial brand dog foods is for cost, rather than dietary needs. These compounds are more commonly known as sugars, and they are seen in simple or complex compounds of carbon, hydrogen, and oxygen. One of the simple sugars is called glucose, and it is vital to many metabolic processes. When large chains of glucose are created, they form compound sugars. One of these is called glycogen, and it is found in the cells of animals. Another, called starch, is the material that is found in the cells of plants.

Carrots are rich in fiber, carbohydrates, and vitamin A. The Carrot Bone™ by Nylabone® is a durable chew containing no plastics or artificial ingredients and can be served as-is, in bone-hard form, or microwaved to a biscuity consistency. Your Rat Terrier will love it.

Vitamins

These are not foods as such but chemical compounds that assist in all aspects of an animal's life. They help in so many ways that to attempt to describe these effectively would require a chapter in itself. Fruits are a rich source of vitamins, as is the liver of most animals. Many vitamins are unstable and easily destroyed by light, heat, moisture, or rancidity. An excess of vitamins, especially A and D, has been proven to be very harmful. Provided a puppy is receiving a balanced diet, it is most unlikely there will be a deficiency, whereas hypervitaminosis (an excess of vitamins) has become quite common due to owners and breeders feeding unneeded supplements. The only time you should feed extra vitamins to your puppy is if your veterinarian advises you to.

Minerals

These provide strength to bone and cell tissue, as well as assist in many metabolic processes. Examples are calcium, phosphorous, copper, iron, magnesium, selenium, potassium, zinc, and sodium. The recommended amounts of all minerals in the diet has not been fully established. Calcium and phosphorous are known to be important, especially to puppies. They help in forming strong bone. As with vitamins, a mineral deficiency is most unlikely in pups given a good and varied diet. Again, an excess can create problems—this applying equally to calcium.

Water

This is the most important of all nutrients, as is easily shown by the fact that the adult dog is made up of about 60 percent water, the puppy containing an even higher percentage. Dogs must retain a water balance, which means that the total intake should be balanced by the total output. The intake comes either by direct input (the tap or its equivalent), plus water released when food is oxidized, known as metabolic water (remember that all foods contain the elements hydrogen and oxygen that recombine in the body to create water). A dog without adequate water will lose condition more rapidly than one depleted of food, a fact common to most animal species.

AMOUNT TO FEED

The best way to determine dietary requirements is by observing the puppy's general health and physical appearance. If he is well covered with flesh, shows good bone development and muscle, and is an active alert puppy, then his diet is fine. A puppy will consume about twice as much as an adult (of the same breed). You should ask the breeder of your puppy to show you the amounts fed to their pups and this will be a good starting point.

The puppy should eat his meal in about five to seven minutes. Any leftover food can be discarded or placed into the refrigerator until the next meal (but be sure it is thawed fully if your fridge is very cold).

If the puppy quickly devours its meal and is clearly still hungry, then you are not giving him enough food. If he eats readily but then begins to

It is fine to give your Rat Terrier treats as long as they are nutritious and do not upset his regular feeding schedule. Owner, Barbara Castro.

pick at it, or walks away leaving a quantity, then you are probably giving him too much food. Adjust this at the next meal and you will quickly begin to appreciate what the correct amount is. If, over a number of weeks, the pup starts to look fat, then he is obviously overeating; the reverse is true if he starts to look thin compared with others of the same breed.

WHEN TO FEED

It really does not matter what times of the day the puppy is fed, as long as he receives the needed quantity of food. Puppies from 8 weeks to 12 or 16 weeks need 3 or 4 meals a day. Older puppies and adult dogs should be fed twice a day. What is most important is that the feeding times are reasonably regular. They can be tailored to fit in with your own timetable—for example, 7 a.m. and 6 p.m. The dog will then expect his meals at these times each day. Keeping regular feeding times and feeding set amounts will help you monitor your puppy's or dog's health. If a dog that's normally enthusiastic about mealtimes and eats readily suddenly shows a lack of interest in food, you'll know something's not right.

TRAINING YOUR RAT TERRIER

Once your puppy has settled into your home and responds to his name, then you can begin his basic training. Before giving advice on how you should go about doing this, two important points should be made. You should train the puppy in isolation of any potential distractions, and you should keep all lessons very short. It is essential that you have the full attention of your puppy. This is not possible if there are other people about, or televisions and radios on, or other pets in the vicinity. Even when the pup has become a young adult, the maximum time you should allocate to a lesson is about 20 minutes. However, you can give the puppy more than one lesson a day, three being as many as are recommended, each well spaced apart.

Praise and the occasional reward are the keys to motivating your Rat Terrier during training sessions.

Accustom your Rat Terrier to wearing his collar as soon as possible.

Before beginning a lesson, always play a little game with the puppy so he is in an active state of mind and thus more receptive to the matter at hand. Likewise, always end a lesson with fun-time for the pup, and always—this is most important—end on a high note, praising the puppy. Let the lesson end when the pup has done as you require so he receives lots of fuss. This will really build his confidence.

COLLAR AND LEASH TRAINING

Training a puppy to his collar and leash is very easy. Place a collar on the puppy and, although he will initially try to bite at it, he will soon forget it, the more so if you play with him. You can leave the collar on for a few hours. Some people leave their dogs' collars on all of the time, others only when they are taking the dog out. If it is to be left on, purchase a narrow or round one so it does not mark the fur.

Once the puppy ignores his collar, then you can attach the leash to it and let the puppy pull this along behind it for a few minutes. However, if the pup starts to chew at the leash, simply hold the leash but keep it slack and let the pup go where he wants. The idea is to let him get the feel of the leash, but not get in the habit of chewing it. Repeat this a couple of times a day for two days and the pup will get used to the leash without thinking that it will restrain him—which you will not have attempted to do yet.

Next, you can let the pup understand that the leash will restrict his movements. The first time he realizes this, he will pull and buck or just sit down. Immediately call the pup to you and give him lots of fuss. Never tug on the leash so the puppy is dragged along the floor, as this simply implants a negative thought in his mind.

Teaching your dog to walk on a leash is one of the first steps in training your Rat Terrier. Noel and Linda Hibbard taking a walk with Bridget and Hercules.

THE COME COMMAND

Come is the most vital of all commands and especially so for the independently minded dog. To teach the puppy to come, let him reach the end of a long lead, then give the command and his name, gently pulling him toward you at the same time. As soon as he associates the word come with the action of moving toward you, pull only when he does not respond immediately. As he starts to come, move back to make him learn that he must come from a distance as well as when he is close to you. Soon you may be able to practice without a leash, but if he is slow to come or notably disobedient, go to him and pull him toward you, repeating the command. Never scold a dog during this exercise—or any other exercise. Remember the trick is that the puppy must want to come to you. For the very independent dog, hand signals may work better than verbal commands.

THE SIT COMMAND

As with most basic commands, your puppy will learn this one in just a few lessons. You can give the puppy two lessons a day on the sit command but he will make just as much progress with one 15-minute lesson each day. Some trainers will advise you that you should not proceed to other commands until the previous one has been learned really well. However, a bright young pup is quite capable of handling more than one command per lesson, and certainly per day. Indeed, as time progresses, you will be going through each command as a matter of routine before a new one is attempted. This is so the puppy always starts, as well as ends, a lesson on a high note, having successfully completed something.

Call the puppy to you and fuss over him. Place one hand on his hindquarters and the other under

With praise, persistence, and practice, your Rat Terrier will soon be sitting on command.

his upper chest. Say "Sit" in a pleasant (never harsh) voice. At the same time, push down his rear end and push up under his chest. Now lavish praise on the puppy. Repeat this a few times and your pet will get the idea. Once the puppy is in the sit position you will release your hands. At first he will tend to get up, so immediately repeat the exercise. The lesson will end when the pup is in the sit position. When the puppy understands the command, and does it right away, you can slowly move backwards so that you are a few feet away from him. If he attempts to come to you, simply place him back in the original position and start again. Do not attempt to keep the pup in the sit position for too long. At this age, even a few seconds is a long while and you do not want him to get bored with lessons before he has even begun them.

THE HEEL COMMAND

All dogs should be able to walk nicely on a leash without their owners being involved in a tug-of-war. The heel command will follow leash training. Heel training is best done where you have a wall to one side of you. This will restrict the puppy's lateral movements, so you only have to contend with forward and backward situations. A fence is an alternative, or you can do the lesson in the garage. Again, it is better to do the lesson in private, not on a public sidewalk where there will be many distractions.

With a puppy, there will be no need to use a choke collar as you can be just as effective with a regular one. The leash should be of good length, certainly not too short. You can adjust the space between you, the

If you are a patient and flexible teacher, the intelligent Rat Terrier can learn the most difficult of tricks. Taxi practices his sit.

The well-mannered and well-trained Rat Terrier will be welcomed anywhere you go and will be able to participate in any activity. This pair poses for a family portrait with owners Carson, Noel and Nolan Hibbard.

puppy, and the wall so your pet has only a small amount of room to move sideways. This being so, he will either hang back or pull ahead—the latter is the more desirable state as it indicates a bold pup who is not frightened of you.

Hold the leash in your right hand and pass it through your left. As the puppy moves ahead and strains on the leash, give the leash a quick jerk backwards with your left hand, at the same time saying "Heel." The position you want the pup to be in is such that his chest is level with, or just behind, an imaginary line from your knee. When the puppy is in this position, praise him and begin walking again, and the whole exercise will be repeated. Once the puppy begins to get the message, you can use your left hand to pat the side of your knee so the pup is encouraged to keep close to your side.

It is useful to suddenly do an about-turn when the pup understands the basics. The puppy will now be behind you, so you can pat your knee and say "Heel." As soon as the pup is in the correct position, give him lots of praise. The puppy will now be beginning to associate certain words with certain actions. Whenever he is not in the heel position he will experience displeasure as you jerk the leash, but when he comes alongside you he will receive praise. Given these two options, he will always prefer the latter—assuming he has no other reason to fear you, which would then create a dilemma in his mind.

Once the lesson has been well learned, then you can adjust your pace from a slow walk to a quick one

Opposite: The athletic and agile Rat Terrier loves to perform for an audience— even an audience of one!

and the puppy will come to adjust. The slow walk is always the more difficult for most puppies, as they are usually anxious to be on the move.

If you have no wall to walk against then things will be a little more difficult because the pup will tend to wander to his left. This means you need to give lateral jerks as well as bring the pup to your side. End the lesson when the pup is walking nicely beside you. Begin the lesson with a few sit commands (which he understands by now), so you're starting with success and praise. If your puppy is nervous on the leash, you should never drag him to your side as you may see so

Don't let that innocent look fool you! Your independent puppy can get into plenty of mischief without the proper training and supervision.

All dogs should learn to walk calmly by your side without pulling. This Rat Terrier practices the heel command.

many other people do (who obviously didn't invest in a good book like you did!). If the pup sits down, call him to your side and give lots of praise. The pup must always come to you because he wants to. If he is dragged to your side he will see you doing the dragging—a big negative. When he races ahead he does not see you jerk the leash, so all he knows is that something restricted his movement and, once he was in a given position, you gave him lots of praise. This is using canine psychology to your advantage.

Always try to remember that if a dog must be disciplined, then try not to let him associate the discipline with you. This is not possible in all matters but, where it is, this is definitely to be preferred.

THE STAY COMMAND

This command follows from the sit. Face the puppy and say "Sit." Now step backwards, and as you do, say "Stay." Let the pup remain in the position for only a few seconds before calling him to you and giving lots of praise. Repeat this, but step further back. You do not need to shout at the puppy. Your pet is not deaf; in fact, his hearing is far better than yours. Speak just loudly enough for the pup to hear, yet use a firm voice. You can stretch the word to form a "sta-a-a-y." If the pup gets up and comes to you simply lift him up, place him back in the original position, and start again. As the pup comes to understand the command, you can move further and further back.

Training classes are a great way to teach your Rat Terrier basic obedience as well as socialize him with other dogs.

The next test is to walk away after placing the pup. This will mean your back is to him, which will tempt him to follow you. Keep an eye over your shoulder, and the minute the pup starts to move, spin around and, using a sterner voice, say either "Sit" or "Stay." If the pup has gotten quite close to you, then, again, return him to the original position.

As the weeks go by you can increase the length of time the pup is left in the stay position—but two to three minutes is quite long enough for a puppy. If your puppy drops into a lying position and is clearly more comfortable, there is nothing wrong with this. Like-wise, your pup will want to face the direction in which you walked off. Some trainers will insist that the dog

————————————————

faces the direction he was placed in, regardless of whether you move off on his blind side. I have never believed in this sort of obedience because it has no practical benefit.

THE DOWN COMMAND

From the puppy's viewpoint, the down command can be one of the more difficult ones to accept. This is because the position is one taken up by a sub-missive dog in a wild pack situation. A timid dog will roll over—a natural gesture of submission. A bolder pup will want to get up, and might back off, not feeling he should have to submit to this command. He will feel that he is under attack from you and about to be punished—which is what would be the position in his natural environment. Once he comes to understand this is not the case, he will accept this unnatural position without any problem.

You may notice that some dogs will sit very quickly, but will respond to the down command more slowly—it is their way of saying that they will obey the command, but under protest!

There are two ways to teach this command. One is, in my mind, more intimidating than the other, but it is up to you to decide which one works best for you. The first method is to stand in front of your puppy and bring him to the sit position, with his collar and leash on. Pass the leash under your left foot so that when you pull on it, the result is that the pup's neck is forced downwards. With your free left hand, push the pup's shoulders down while at the same time saying "Down." This is when a bold pup will instantly try to back off and wriggle in full protest. Hold the pup firmly by the shoulders so he stays in the position for a second or two, then tell him what a good dog he is and give him lots of praise. Repeat this only a few times in a lesson because otherwise the puppy will get bored and upset over this command. End with an easy command that brings back the pup's confidence.

The second method, and the one I prefer, is done as follows: Stand in front of the pup and then tell him to sit. Now kneel down, which is immediately far less intimidating to the puppy than to have you towering above him. Take each of his front legs and pull them forward, at the same time saying "Down." Release the legs and quickly apply light pressure on the shoulders with your left hand. Then, as quickly, say "Good boy" and give lots of fuss. Repeat two or three times only. The pup will learn over a few lessons. Remember, this is a very submissive act on the pup's behalf, so there is no need to rush matters.

RECALL TO HEEL COMMAND

When your puppy is coming to the heel position from an off-leash situation—such as if he has been running free—he should do this in the correct manner. He should pass behind you and take up his position and then sit. To teach this command, have the pup in front of you in the sit position with his collar and leash on. Hold the leash in your right hand. Give him the command to heel, and pat your left knee. As the pup starts to move forward, use your right hand to guide him behind you. If need be you can hold his collar and walk the dog around the back of you to the desired position. You will need to repeat this a few times until the dog understands what is wanted.

When he has done this a number of times, you can try it without the collar and leash. If the pup comes up toward your left side, then bring him to the sit position in front of you, hold his collar and walk him around the back of you. He will eventually understand and automatically pass around your back each time. If the dog is already behind you when you recall him, then he should automatically come to your left side, which you will be patting with your hand.

THE NO COMMAND

This is a command that must be obeyed every time without fail. There are no halfway stages, he must be 100-percent reliable. Most delinquent dogs have never been taught this command; included in these are the jumpers, the barkers, and the biters. Were your puppy to approach a poisonous snake or any other potential danger, the no command, coupled with the recall, could save his life. You do not need to give a specific lesson for this command because it will crop up time and again in day-to-day life.

If the puppy is chewing a slipper, you should approach the pup, take hold of the slipper, and say "No" in a stern voice. If he jumps onto the furniture, lift him off and say "No" and place him gently on the floor. You must be consistent in the use of the command and apply it every time he is doing something you do not want him to do.

YOUR HEALTHY RAT TERRIER

Dogs, like all other animals, are capable of contracting problems and diseases that, in most cases, are easily avoided by sound husbandry—meaning well-bred and well-cared-for animals are less prone to developing diseases and problems than are carelessly bred and neglected animals. Your knowledge of how to avoid problems is far more valuable than all of the books and advice on how to cure them. Respectively, the only person you should listen to about treatment is your vet. Veterinarians don't have all the answers, but at least they are trained to analyze and treat illnesses, and are aware of the full implications of treatments. This does not mean a few old remedies aren't good standbys when all else fails, but in most cases modern science provides the best treatments for disease.

Opposite: As a responsible Rat Terrier owner, you should have a basic understanding of the medical problems that effect the breed.

PHYSICAL EXAMS

Your puppy should receive regular physical examinations or check-ups. These come in two forms. One is obviously performed by your vet, and the other is a day-to-day procedure that should be done by you. Apart from the fact the exam will highlight any problem at an early stage, it is an excellent way of socializing the pup to being handled.

To do the physical exam yourself, start at the head and work your way around the body. You are looking for any sign of lesions, or any indication of parasites on the pup. The most common parasites are fleas and ticks.

HEALTHY TEETH AND GUMS

Chewing is instinctual. Puppies chew so that their teeth and jaws grow strong and healthy as they develop. As the permanent teeth begin to emerge, it is painful and annoying to the puppy, and puppy owners must recognize that their new charges

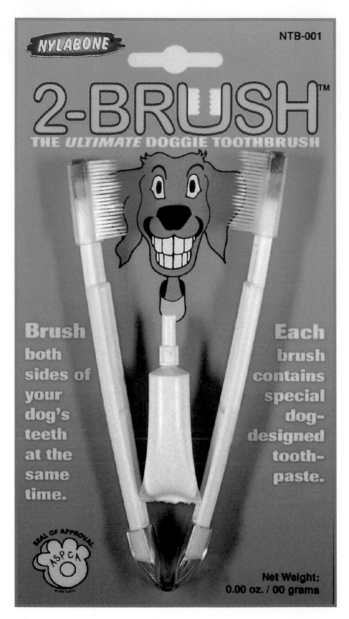

As a pet owner, it is essential to keep your dog's teeth clean by removing surface tartar and plaque. 2-Brush™ by Nylabone® is made with two toothbrushes to clean both sides of your dog's teeth at the same time. Each brush contains a toothpaste reservoir designed to apply the toothpaste, which is specially formulated for dogs, directly into the brush.

need something safe upon which to chew. Unfortunately, once the puppy's permanent teeth have emerged and settled solidly into the jaw, the chewing instinct does not fade. Adult dogs instinctively need to clean their teeth, massage their gums, and exercise their jaws through chewing.

It is necessary for your dog to have clean teeth. You should take your dog to the veterinarian at least once a year to have his teeth cleaned and to have his mouth examined for any sign of oral disease. Although dogs do not get cavities in the same way humans do, dogs'

The Hercules® by Nylabone® has raised dental tips that help fight plaque on your Rat Terrier's teeth and gums.

teeth accumulate tartar, and more quickly than humans do! Veterinarians recommend brushing your dog's teeth daily. But who can find time to brush their dog's teeth daily? The accumulation of tartar and plaque on our dog's teeth when not removed can cause irritation and eventually erode the enamel and finally destroy the teeth. Advanced cases, while destroying the teeth, bring on gingivitis and periodontitis, two very serious conditions that can affect the dog's internal organs as well...to say nothing about bad breath!

Since everyone can't brush their dog's teeth daily or get to the veterinarian often enough for him to scale

Nylafloss® does wonders for your Rat Terrier's dental health by massaging his gums and literally flossing between his teeth, loosening plaque and tartar build-up. Unlike cotton tug toys, Nylafloss® won't rot or fray.

the dog's teeth, providing the dog with something safe to chew on will help maintain oral hygeine. Chew devices from Nylabone® keep dogs' teeth clean, but they also provide an excellent resource for entertainment and relief of doggie tensions. Nylabone® products give your dog something to do for an hour or two every day and during that hour or two, your dog will be taking an active part in keeping his teeth and gums healthy…without even realizing it! That's invaluable to your dog, and valuable to you!

Nylabone® provides fun bones, challenging bones, and *safe* bones. It is an owner's responsibility to recognize safe chew toys from dangerous ones. Your dog will chew and devour anything you give him. Dogs must not be permitted to chew on items that they can break. Pieces of broken objects can do internal damage to a dog, besides ripping the dog's mouth. Cheap plastic or rubber toys can cause stoppage in the intestines; such stoppages are operable only if caught immediately.

Nylabone® is the only plastic dog bone made of 100% virgin nylon, specially processed to create a tough, durable, completely safe bone.

The most obvious choices, in this case, may be the worst choice. Natural beef bones were not designed for chewing and cannot take too much pressure from the sides. Due to the abrasive nature of these bones, they should be offered most sparingly. Knuckle bones, though once very popular for dogs, can be easily

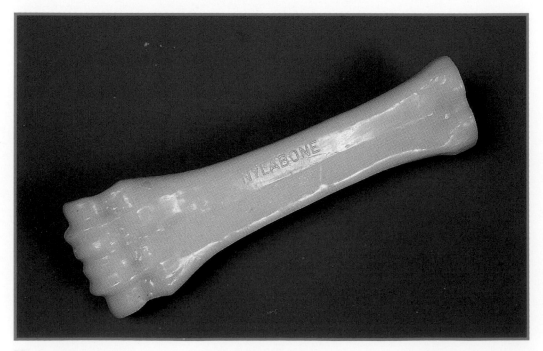

Chick-n-Cheez Chooz® are completely safe and nutritious health chews made from pure cheese protein, chicken, and fortified with vitamin E. They contain no salt, sugar, plastic, or preservatives and less than 1% fat.

chewed up and eaten by dogs. At the very least, digestion is interrupted; at worst, the dog can choke or suffer from intestinal blockage.

When a dog chews hard on a Nylabone®, little bristle-like projections appear on the surface of the bone. These help to clean the dog's teeth and add to the gum-massaging. Given the chemistry of the nylon, the bristle can pass through the dog's intestinal tract without effect. Since nylon is inert, no microorganism can grow on it, and it can be washed in soap and water or sterilized in boiling water or in an autoclave.

For the sake of your dog, his teeth and your own peace of mind, provide your dog with Nylabones®. They have 100 variations from which to choose.

FIGHTING FLEAS

Fleas are very mobile and may be red, black, or brown in color. The adults suck the blood of the host, while the larvae feed on the feces of the adults, which is rich in blood. Flea "dirt" may be seen on the pup as very tiny clusters of blackish specks that look like freshly ground pepper. The eggs of fleas may be laid on the puppy, though they are more commonly laid off the host in a favorable place, such as the bedding. They normally hatch in 4 to 21 days, depending on the temperature, but they can survive for up to 18 months if temperature conditions are not favorable. The larvae are maggot-like and molt a couple of times before forming pupae, which can survive long periods until the temperature, or the vibration of a nearby host, causes them to emerge and jump on a host.

There are a number of effective treatments available, and you should discuss them with your veterinarian, then follow all instructions for the one you choose. Any treatment will involve a product for your puppy or dog and one for the environment, and will require diligence on your part to treat all areas and thoroughly clean your home and yard until the infestation is eradicated.

THE TROUBLE WITH TICKS

Ticks are arthropods of the spider family, which means they have eight legs (though the larvae have six). They bury their headparts into the host and gorge on its blood. They are easily seen as small grain-like creatures sticking out from the skin. They are often picked up when dogs play in fields, but may also arrive in your yard via wild animals—even birds—or stray cats and dogs. Some ticks are species-specific, others are more adaptable and will host on many species.

The cat flea is the most common flea of dogs. It starts feeding soon after it makes contact with the dog.

The deer tick is the most common carrier of Lyme disease. Photo courtesy of Virbac Laboratories, Inc., Fort Worth, Texas.

The most troublesome type of tick is the deer tick, which spreads the deadly Lyme disease that can cripple a dog (or a person). Deer ticks are tiny and very hard to detect. Often, by the time they're big enough to notice, they've been feeding on the dog for a few days—long enough to do their damage. Lyme disease was named for the area of the United States in which it was first detected—Lyme, Connecticut—but has now been diagnosed in almost all parts of the U.S. Your veterinarian can advise you of the danger to your dog(s) in your area, and may suggest your dog be vaccinated for Lyme. Always go over your dog with a fine-toothed flea comb when you come in from walking through any area that may harbor deer ticks, and if your dog is acting unusually sluggish or sore, seek veterinary advice.

Attempts to pull a tick free will invariably leave the headpart in the pup, where it will die and cause an infected wound or abscess. The best way to remove ticks is to dab a strong saline solution, iodine, or alcohol on them. This will numb them, causing them to loosen their hold, at which time they can be removed with forceps. The wound can then be cleaned and covered with an antiseptic ointment. If ticks are common in your area, consult with your vet for a suitable pesticide to be used in kennels, on bedding, and on the puppy or dog.

INSECTS AND OTHER OUTDOOR DANGERS

There are many biting insects, such as mosquitoes, that can cause discomfort to a puppy. Many diseases are transmitted by the males of these species.

A pup can easily get a grass seed or thorn lodged between his pads or in the folds of his ears. These may go unnoticed until an abscess forms.

This is where your daily check of the puppy or dog will do a world of good. If your puppy has been playing in long grass or places where there may be thorns, pine needles, wild animals, or parasites, the check-up is a wise precaution.

There are many parasites, such as fleas and ticks, that your dog can encounter, so closely supervise him when he is outside.

SKIN DISORDERS

Apart from problems associated with lesions created by biting pests, a puppy may fall foul to a number of other skin disorders. Examples are ringworm, mange, and eczema. Ringworm is not caused by a worm, but is a fungal infection. It manifests itself as a sore-looking bald circle. If your puppy should have any form of bald patches, let your veterinarian check him over; a microscopic examination can confirm the condition. Many old remedies for ringworm exist, such as iodine, carbolic acid, formalin, and other tinctures, but modern drugs are superior.

Fungal infections can be very difficult to treat, and even more difficult to eradicate, because of the spores. These can withstand most treatments, other than burning, which is the best thing to do with bedding once the condition has been confirmed.

Mange is a general term that can be applied to many skin conditions where the hair falls out and a flaky crust develops and falls away.

Often, dogs will scratch themselves, and this invariably is worse than the original condition, for it opens lesions that are then subject to viral, fungal, or parasitic attack. The cause of the problem can be various species of mites. These either live on skin debris and the hair follicles, which they destroy, or they bury themselves just beneath the skin and feed on the tissue. Applying general remedies from pet stores is not recommended because it is essential to identify the type of mange before a specific treatment is effective.

Eczema is another non-specific term applied to many skin disorders. The condition can be brought about in many ways. Sunburn, chemicals, allergies to foods, drugs, pollens, and even stress can all produce a deterioration of the skin and coat. Given the range of causal factors, treatment can be difficult because the problem is one of identification. It is a case of taking each possibility at a time and trying to correctly diagnose the matter. If the cause is of a dietary nature then you must remove one item at a time in order to find out if the dog is allergic to a given food. It could, of course, be the lack of a nutrient that is the problem, so if the condition persists, you should consult your veterinarian.

INTERNAL DISORDERS

It cannot be overstressed that it is very foolish to attempt to diagnose an internal disorder without the advice of a veterinarian. Take a relatively common problem such as diarrhea. It might be caused by nothing more serious than the puppy hogging a lot of food or eating something that it has never previously eaten. Conversely, it could be the first indication of a potentially fatal disease. It's up to your veterinarian to make the correct diagnosis.

The following symptoms, especially if they accompany each other or are progressively added to earlier symptoms, mean you should visit the veterinarian right away:

Continual vomiting. All dogs vomit from time to time and this is not necessarily a sign of illness. They will eat grass to induce vomiting. It is a natural cleansing process common to many carnivores. However, continued vomiting is a clear sign of a problem. It may be a blockage in the pup's intestinal tract, it may be induced by worms, or it could be due to any number of diseases.

Diarrhea. This, too, may be nothing more than a temporary condition due to many factors. Even a change of home can induce diarrhea, because this often stresses the pup, and invariably there is some change in the diet. If it persists more than 48 hours then something is amiss. If blood is seen in the feces, waste no time at all in taking the dog to the vet.

Running eyes and/or nose. A pup might have a chill and this will cause the eyes and nose to weep. Again, this should quickly clear up if the puppy is placed in a warm environment and away from any drafts. If it does not, and especially if a mucous discharge is seen, then the pup has an illness that must be diagnosed.

Coughing. Prolonged coughing is a sign of a problem, usually of a respiratory nature.

Wheezing. If the pup has difficulty breathing and makes a wheezing sound when breathing, then something is wrong.

Cries when attempting to defecate or urinate. This might only be a minor problem due to the hard state of the feces, but it could be more serious, especially if the pup cries when urinating.

Cries when touched. Obviously, if you do not handle a puppy with care he might yelp. However, if he cries even when lifted gently, then he has an internal problem that becomes apparent when pressure is applied to a given area of the body. Clearly, this must be diagnosed.

Refuses food. Generally, puppies and dogs are greedy creatures when it comes to feeding time. Some might be more fussy, but none should refuse more than one meal. If they go for a number of hours without showing any interest in their food, then something is not as it should be.

General listlessness. All puppies have their off days when they do not seem their usual cheeky, mischievous selves. If this condition persists for more than two days then there is little doubt of a problem. They may not show any of the signs listed, other than perhaps a reduced interest in their food. There are many diseases that can develop internally without displaying obvious clinical signs. Blood, fecal, and other tests are needed in order to identify the disorder before it reaches an advanced state that may not be treatable.

WORMS

There are many species of worms, and a number of these live in the tissues of dogs and most other animals. Many create no problem at all, so you are not even aware they exist. Others can be tolerated in small levels, but become a major problem if they number more than a few. The most common types coon in dogs are roundworms and tapeworms. While roundworms are the greater problem, tapeworms require an intermediate host so are more easily eradicated.

Roundworms are spaghetti-like worms that cause a pot-bellied appearance and dull coat, along with more severe symptoms, such as diarrhea and vomiting. Photo courtesy of Merck AgVet.

Roundworms of the species *Toxocara canis* infest the dog. They may grow to a length of 8 inches (20 cm) and look like strings of spaghetti. The worms feed on the digesting food in the pup's intestines. In chronic cases the puppy will become pot-bellied, have diarrhea, and will vomit. Eventually, he will stop eating, having passed through the stage when he always seems hungry. The worms lay eggs in the puppy and these pass out in his feces. They are then either ingested by the pup, or they are eaten by mice, rats, or beetles. These may then be eaten by the puppy and the life cycle is complete.

Larval worms can migrate to the womb of a pregnant bitch, or to her mammary glands, and this is how they pass to the puppy. The pregnant bitch can be wormed, which will help. The pups can, and should,

Whipworms are hard to find unless you strain your dog's feces, and this is best left to a veterinarian. Pictured here are adult whipworms.

be wormed when they are about two weeks old. Repeat worming every 10 to 14 days and the parasites should be removed. Worms can be extremely dangerous to young puppies, so you should be sure the pup is wormed as a matter of routine.

Tapeworms can be seen as tiny rice-like eggs sticking to the puppy's or dog's anus. They are less destructive, but still undesirable. The eggs are eaten by mice, fleas, rabbits, and other animals that serve as intermediate hosts. They develop into a larval stage and the host must be eaten by the dog in order to complete the chain. Your vet will supply a suitable remedy if tapeworms are seen or suspected. There are other worms, such as hookworms and whipworms, that are also blood suckers. They will make a pup anemic, and blood might be seen in the feces, which can be examined by the vet to confirm their presence. Cleanliness in all matters is the best preventative measure for all worms.

Heartworm infestation in dogs is passed by mosquitoes but can be prevented by a monthly (or daily) treatment that is given orally. Talk to your vet about the risk of heartworm in your area.

BLOAT (GASTRIC DILATATION)

This condition has proved fatal in many dogs, especially large and deep-chested breeds, such as the Weimaraner and the Great Dane. However, any dog can get bloat. It is caused by swallowing air during exercise, food/water gulping or another strenuous task. As many believe, it is not the result of flatulence. The stomach of an affected dog twists, disallowing food and blood flow and resulting in harmful toxins being released into the bloodstream. Death can easily follow if the condition goes undetected.

The best preventative measure is not to feed large meals or exercise your puppy or dog immediately after he has eaten. Veterinarians recommend feeding three smaller meals per day in an elevated feeding rack, adding water to dry food to prevent gulping, and not offering water during mealtimes.

VACCINATIONS

Every puppy, purebred or mixed breed, should be vaccinated against the major canine diseases. These are distemper, leptospirosis, hepatitis, and canine parvovirus. Your puppy may have received a temporary vaccination against distemper before you purchased him, but be sure to ask the breeder to be sure.

The age at which vaccinations are given can vary, but will usually be when the pup is 8 to 12 weeks old. By this time any protection given to the pup by antibodies received from his mother via her initial milk feeds will be losing their strength.

Rely on your veterinarian for the most effectual vaccination schedule for your Rat Terrier puppy.

The puppy's immune system works on the basis that the white blood cells engulf and render harmless

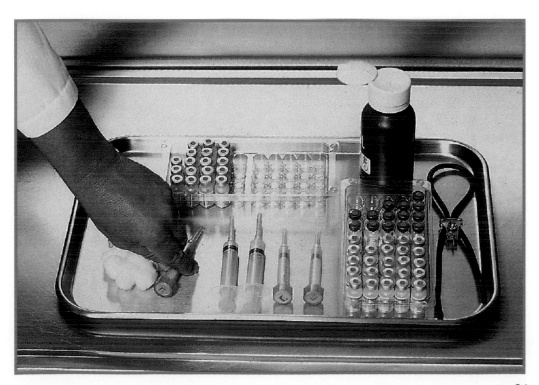

attacking bacteria. However, they must first recognize a potential enemy.

Vaccines are either dead bacteria or they are live, but in very small doses. Either type prompts the pup's defense system to attack them. When a large attack then comes (if it does), the immune system recognizes it and massive numbers of lymphocytes (white blood corpuscles) are mobilized to counter the attack. However, the ability of the cells to recognize these dangerous viruses can diminish over a period of time. It is therefore useful to provide annual reminders about the nature of the enemy. This is done by means of booster injections that keep the immune system on its alert. Immunization is not 100-percent guaranteed to be successful, but is very close. Certainly it is better than giving the puppy no protection.

Dogs are subject to other viral attacks, and if these are of a high-risk factor in your area, then your vet will suggest you have the puppy vaccinated against these as well.

Your puppy or dog should also be vaccinated against the deadly rabies virus. In fact, in many places it is illegal for your dog not to be vaccinated. This is to protect your dog, your family, and the rest of the animal population from this deadly virus that infects the nervous system and causes dementia and death.

ACCIDENTS

All puppies will get their share of bumps and bruises due to the rather energetic way they play. These will usually heal themselves over a few days. Small cuts should be bathed with a suitable disinfectant and then smeared with an antiseptic ointment. If a cut looks more serious, then stem the flow of blood with a towel or makeshift tourniquet and rush the pup to the veterinarian. Never apply so much pressure to the wound that it might restrict the flow of blood to the limb.

In the case of burns you should apply cold water or an ice pack to the surface. If the burn was due to a chemical, then this must be washed away with copious amounts of water. Apply petroleum jelly, or any vegetable oil, to the burn. Trim away the hair if need be. Wrap the dog in a blanket and rush him to the vet. The pup may go into shock, depending on the severity of the burn, and this will result in a lowered blood pressure, which is dangerous and the reason the pup must receive immediate veterinary attention.

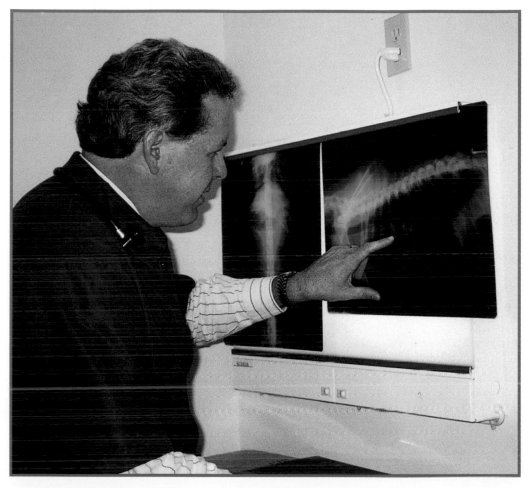

It is a good idea to x-ray the chest and abdomen on any dog hit by a car.

If a broken limb is suspected then try to keep the animal as still as possible. Wrap your pup or dog in a blanket to restrict movement and get him to the veterinarian as soon as possible. Do not move the dog's head so it is tilting backward, as this might result in blood entering the lungs.

Do not let your pup jump up and down from heights, as this can cause considerable shock to the joints. Like all youngsters, puppies do not know when enough is enough, so you must do all their thinking for them.

Provided you apply strict hygiene to all aspects of raising your puppy, and you make daily checks on his physical state, you have done as much as you can to safeguard him during his most vulnerable period. Routine visits to your veterinarian are also recommended, especially while the puppy is under one year of age. The vet may notice something that did not seem important to you.

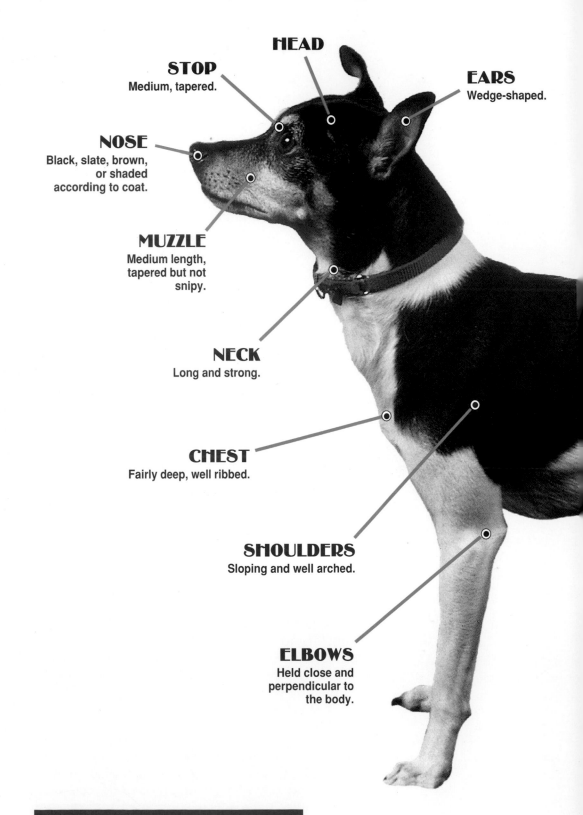

HEAD

STOP
Medium, tapered.

EARS
Wedge-shaped.

NOSE
Black, slate, brown,
or shaded
according to coat.

MUZZLE
Medium length,
tapered but not
snipy.

NECK
Long and strong.

CHEST
Fairly deep, well ribbed.

SHOULDERS
Sloping and well arched.

ELBOWS
Held close and
perpendicular to
the body.

Rat Terrier photographed by Isabelle Francais.